Praise for Dubravka Ugresic

"Like Nabokov, Ugresic affirms our ability to remember as a source for saving our moral and compassionate identity."—John Balaban, *Washington Post*

"A genuinely free-thinker, Ugresic's attachment to absurdity leads her down paths where other writers fear to tread."—*The Independent*

"As long as some, like Ugresic, who can write well, do, there will be hope for the future."—*New Criterion*

"Ugresic's wit is bound by no preconceived purposes, and once the story takes off, a wild freedom of association and adventurous discernment is set in motion. . . . Ugresic dissects the social world."
—*World Literature Today*

"Never has a writer been more aware of how one narrative depends on another."—Joanna Walsh

"Ugresic must be numbered among what Jacques Maritain called the dreamers of the true; she draws us into the dream."—*New York Times*

"Ugresic is also affecting and eloquent, in part because within her quirky, aggressively sweet plot she achieves moments of profundity and evokes the stoicism innate in such moments."—Mary Gaitskill

"Dubravka Ugresic is the philosopher of evil and exile, and the storyteller of many shattered lives."—Charles Simic

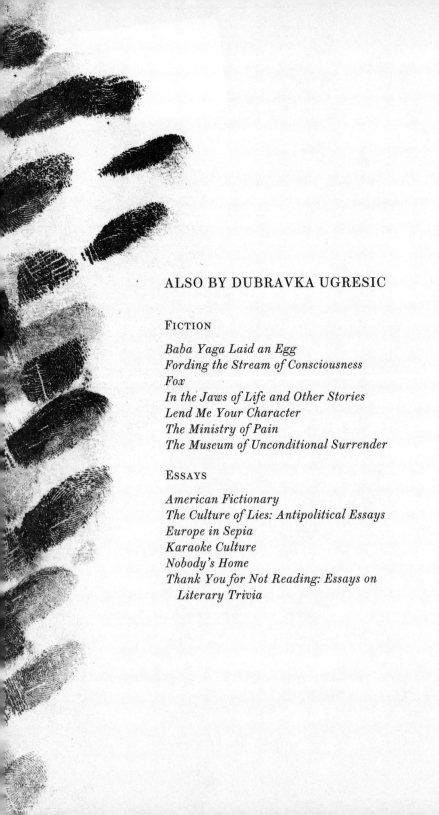

ALSO BY DUBRAVKA UGRESIC

FICTION

ESSAYS

THE AGE
OF SKIN

DUBRAVKA UGRESIC

Translated from the Croatian
by Ellen Elias-Bursać

OPEN LETTER
LITERARY TRANSLATIONS FROM THE UNIVERSITY OF ROCHESTER

First edition, 2020
All rights reserved

Library of Congress Cataloging-in-Publication Data: Available.
ISBN-13: 978-1-948830-22-5 | ISBN-10: 1-948830-22-1

*This project is supported in part by an award from the National Endowment for the
Arts and the New York State Council on the Arts with the support of
Governor Andrew M. Cuomo and the New York State Legislature.*

Printed on acid-free paper in the United States of America.

Cover Design by Jack Smyth
Interior Design by Anthony Blake

Open Letter is the University of Rochester's nonprofit, literary translation press:
Dewey Hall 1-219, Box 278968, Rochester, NY 14627

www.openletterbooks.org

Contents

THE AGE OF SKIN

And on his way he met a man who was, with his breath, turning a millstone. The young man stood and watched. Then he stepped closer and inquired:

"What are you doing?"

"I'm grinding up people."

Roma fairy tale

The Age of Skin

And so for a long, long time, Snow White lay there, always as fresh as she'd been when alive, she still appeared to be sleeping; all her beauty remained, for she was, as ever, white as snow, red as a rose, and her hair, black as ebony.

Brothers Grimm, "Snow White and the Seven Dwarves"

1.

I shudder when I hear the hackneyed (and strident) line that *life writes novels*. Let's be clear: if life wrote novels, there'd be no such thing as fiction. Literature may be on its last legs, but its infirmity is due not to the historic ascendance of life over literature but to literature's own self-destruction, brought about through the earnest efforts of the very people who propel the literary process: the avaricious publishers, laggardly editors, wishy-washy critics, unambitious readers, and authors lacking in talent but greedy for fame. As to the relationship between literature and life, things stand, more or less, as follows: gossip lies at the heart of the literary story. We all love to know what happens to others, even what they ate for lunch. Big-time novels are, also, big-time gossip mills. Has this changed with the advent of new media? No, indeed, the appetite for gossip has only mushroomed. Gossipmongers tweet, text, like, post. Social networks are their natural habitat. *Reality* literature—delving with minute detail into the private lives of celebrities—has now reached its apotheosis. The earlier hagiographies on the lives of the saints have now evolved, genre-wise, into biographies, autobiographies, and memoirs. Once the greed for gossip has been whetted, putting a stop to it is a challenge. All of us are now saints. We flay our own skin, readily expose our inner organs; each of us is on display in the shop window at the local butcher's.

2.

English has a wealth of skin-related phrases: To *have thick* or *thin skin, get under someone's skin, jump out of one's skin, escape by the skin of your teeth, save your skin, strip down to the bare skin*, and sayings such as *beauty's only skin-deep, no skin off my nose, no skin in the game, skinflint, skinny-dipping* . . . Skin is intimate, and, as far as intimacy goes, it takes precedence over metaphors of the heart. While our heart is poised to love all of humanity, we are loved only by our skin.

The Slavic languages do not have distinct words for the two kinds of skin like English (*skin, leather*), or German (*haut, leder*), or Dutch (*huid, leer*), or Spanish (*piel, cuero*) or, for example, Italian (*pelle, cuoio*). Many Slavs use the same word for both our body's envelope and the material used to cobble shoes. Perhaps this absence of linguistic diversity has to do with differences in civilization? Might this lapse in articulation be the source of the obsession with "genuine leather" among a certain class of shoppers?

Ex-Yugoslavs in the second half of the twentieth century traveled to neighboring Italy, to Trieste, to buy shoes, purses, and jackets (made, of course, of *genuine* leather). Later they trotted off to more affordable Istanbul and lugged leather clothing back to the Yugoslav flea markets. A man wearing a leather jacket and a gold chain around his neck was generally seen as a good catch. When the popularity of *genuine* leather was at its peak, the feeling was that a man wearing a leather jacket was ready for anything. Soon, cheap imitations eroded the appeal of genuine leather, and human males and females wearing leather jackets slipped for a time into the socially stigmatized human niche: "trash." And leather slipped into a leather subculture where it became the "empress," a fetish, a cult.

3.

Like all intellectuals with a humanistic bent, I drop to my knees before science. There is no one who can wow me more than mathematicians, physicists, astronomers, physicians, and statisticians; nobody can place things in their true perspective the way they can. So, an article was recently published in the Croatian press with the provocative title, "Countries with a fat population, like Croatia, are a burden to Earth." Apparently, the United States holds first place as the fattest country in the world, with Croatia coming in third, right behind Kuwait. Among the skinniest are the Asian and African countries, with North Korea in first place. The article quotes a recent study published in the journal *BMC Public Health*, which claims that the average mass of an adult on Earth is 136 pounds (significantly greater in the U.S.: 177.9 pounds). When all is added up, the world's adult population now weighs 287 million tons, of which 15 million tons are due to overweight people, and 3.5 million tons are due to obesity. Fat is distributed unequally: the people of the United States comprise only five percent of the world's population, yet account for one third of the human biomass. Professor Ian Roberts says scientists today think not about how many mouths there are to feed, but how much flesh there is. "Everyone accepts that population growth threatens global environmental sustainability—our study shows that population fatness is also a serious threat. Unless we tackle both population and fatness, our chances are slim," says Professor Roberts. The problem, therefore, is in the meat, in human flesh.

The stigmatization of fat people has found support in branches of science such as demography and ecology, medicine and socio-economics. Medicine has posited that obesity may, in fact, be contagious (the discovery of the Ad36 virus): those who fraternize with the obese may, themselves, become obese. Adele, a generously proportioned British singer, was criticized on several local TV stations in the United States during her tour. A local fitness instructor, as full of righteous indignation as only fitness instructors can be, claimed that Adele was a threat to the United States because she was sending a message to young American girls that one could be overweight and yet have great success as a singer, which was not—in the fitness instructor's humble opinion—the message young girls should be hearing. Who knows, perhaps in the near future similar words will be heard when open season is declared on a future Adele, who will be promptly sent back to where she first dared let loose her divine voice, to the ghetto of the poor, the fat, and the talented.

4.

At one moment in history, men in black leather coats could do almost anything, but since then they have been all but forgotten. The book *Lenin's Embalmers*[1] is an unusual case of testimony about the dermis of the famous revolutionary who was the symbol of one of the greatest, the most thrilling, and perhaps, for that very reason, most catastrophic social experiments in the history of mankind. Ilya Zbarsky is the son of Boris Zbarsky, a Soviet biochemist who, with Professor Vorobyov, embalmed Lenin. Ilya Zbarsky, himself a biochemist, worked with the team of experts at Lenin's Mausoleum in Moscow for nearly twenty years. His story offers astonishing insight into the long life of a mummy, but also into the lives of the people who were involved in preserving it.

The most fascinating parts of the book are the descriptions of salvaging Lenin's skin, and the constant attention to its possible deterioration. We can only imagine how this whole team of top experts must have felt when, only two months after the (initial) embalming of Lenin's body, the special commission for assessing the condition of Lenin's corpse reported:

"The corpse had turned sallow, with more marked discoloration

---

1 Ilya Zbarsky & Samuel Hutchinson, *Lenin's Embalmers*, The Harvill Press, 1998.

around the eyes, nose, ears and temples. Wrinkles and a purplish stain had appeared over the frontal and parietal lobes of the brain. The tip of the nose was covered in dark pigments, and the walls of the nostrils had become paper thin; the eyes were half open and sinking into their sockets; the lips had parted, leaving the teeth clearly visible; brown spots had appeared on the hands, and the fingernails were tinged with blue."[2]

After this alarming report, Lenin's lungs, liver, and other internal organs were removed, his eyeballs replaced with artificial ones, the inside of the body rinsed with distilled water and a powerful antiseptic, the body treated with formaldehyde, acetic acid, alcohol, glycerin, chloride, and other chemicals. This saved Lenin's skin, and the lives, at least most of the lives, of the scientists on the team. Among the many unexplained deaths from those years was the death of Professor Vorobyov, the principal inventor of the Soviet method of embalming.

One of the "poignant" moments of the book is about Nadezhda Krupskaya (Lenin's wife) who, with a woman's regret, conceded—when she visited the Mausoleum in 1938—that Lenin still had a youthful look, while she had, meanwhile, aged.

By 1945, the original 1939 team of four scientists swelled to thirty-five top histologists, anatomists, biochemists, physicians, and others. Together they researched the structure of skin and subcutaneous tissue cells, and the autolytic factors causing tissue deterioration. Between 1949 and 1995, the institute associated

---

2 Ibid. p. 79.

with the Lenin Mausoleum stepped into the international arena and embalmed the bodies of Georgi Dimitrov, Klement Gottwald, Ho Chi Minh, Agostinho Neto, Linden Forbes Burnham, Kim Il Sung, and Mongolian dictator Khorloogiin Choibalsan. By the 1990s, most of these famous mummies had been cremated or buried. Stalin's mummy, after being displayed next to Lenin's for nearly a decade, was cremated as well.

The Lenin's Mausoleum team was not disbanded; instead it continued with its work, but now as a high-end funeral parlor. The customers of their costly services today are the wealthy of Russia and various underworld figures. Today, the embalmers use the same solvents as were used in the fluid for embalming Lenin, and they pump the same eight liters of these into the veins of the dead. The embalming is so effective that the body remains unchanged for as long as a year after burial. Ilya Zbarsky says that after injecting the embalming fluid into the veins, the skin of the deceased promptly changes from the bluish hue of a corpse to the color of ivory. In other words, someone who had a poor complexion during their lifetime may see it improved in death.

Today, Lenin's Mausoleum, as an upscale funeral parlor, also sells caskets. The most sought after are the ones labeled "Made in USA." The most expensive are the Russian caskets made of precious crystal, and the most popular is the "Al Capone," a model copied from the casket seen in *The Godfather*.[3]

---

3 Apparently, since the demise of Communism, many morticians in the death industry have shown a creative flair. Zbigniew Lindner, of Poland, thought to enliven the business image of his casket-manufacturing company with photographs in his catalogue of caskets displayed with naked models, which appalled the more fervent Catholics among the Poles. "Our intention was to let people know that a casket

As to Lenin's mummy, its fate has been the subject of debate for several years now, and still there is no resolution. Russian newspapers and online forums reignite the discussion now and then, but only a smattering of voices air opinions for and against the Mausoleum.

5.

Peter van der Helm, proprietor of a tattoo parlor in Amsterdam, came up with the idea of purchasing pieces of tattooed skin. "Everyone spends their lives in search of immortality and this is a simple way to get a piece of it," van der Helm announced. His parlor is called *Walls and Skin*, and dozens of van der Helm's clients have already bequeathed their skin to the recently established foundation; they each pay several hundred euros for the procedure. When a client dies, a pathologist removes the patch of skin with the tattoo and sends it off for further processing. Floris Hirschfeld, a client, says: "People have animals stuffed and mounted in their homes, so why not skin? (. . .) If I can be preserved like this, yes, please." And besides, "some people mean so much to me that I want them with me always, and this is a way to accomplish this," says Hirschfeld, who had a portrait of his late mother tattooed on his back. "Vincent van Gogh was a poor man when he died. You and I can't buy a Van Gogh. Tattooing is the people's form of art," he adds.

---

needn't be a sacred object. Instead, I see it as a piece of furniture, the last bed you'll sleep on. It is not a religious symbol. It's a commodity," said Zbigniew, and added: "We decided to present both the beauty of Polish women and our caskets. So much effort is invested in them, yet they are seen only at the funeral."

6.

When we examine the cultural landscape surrounding us now, we begin to feel that focusing on any one thing is difficult because of the colorful array of shapes and objects. Yet if we look more closely and if, of course, hold off from snorting scornfully at ubiquitous popular culture, we might see that in this landscape now stripped of a divine hierarchy, what dominates is human flesh. The theme of human flesh under threat has long been a favorite topic of popular culture; it was the "outsiders," the aliens, vampires, zombies, and cannibals, who chomped on human skin. We find this in genre novels, comic strips, video games, and movies, and, together with a slenderer corpus of serious work, they join to build a modern mythical field for readers, building on contemporary human fears—primarily a fear for one's own skin. The trilogy of *The Hunger Games* by Suzanne Collins (the American version of an earlier novel, *Battle Royale*, by Koushun Takami) owes its popularity to a harshly draconian message: if the human individual is to preserve its own skin today, that individual will have to kill other individuals. There is a similar message in Kazuo Ishiguro's novel *Never Let Me Go* (and the screen version as well), where the world is divided into the "clones" (donors), and "normal people." A similar message is developed by Ewan McGregor and Scarlett Johansson, who play characters in *The Island*. The two of them are "harvestable beings," human clones designated for the "organ harvest."

For most people, popular-culture themes allow them to get a reading of their current reality and a sense of an imminent future. The hunt for human organs, for example, wrapped in protective, religious-philanthropic cellophane, does, actually, exist, and the boundaries set to limit what is allowed in this arena are shifting with each passing day. The rule that organs must be harvested only from donors who have died—a practice that shocks nobody anymore—has expanded to include living donors, and then to the illegal sale of one's own organs (from blood, and so on) for the purpose of extending life. In the mythical story about organs, only the donor is (at least partially) disclosed, while the recipient remains hidden. The unnamed recipient, through illegal dealers, buys or takes whatever organs are needed, without examining their own ethical position. So it is that the boundaries limiting what is permissible spread to the point of ghoulish theft, such as in the recent news of a Chinese six-year-old who disappeared, only to be found several hours later, lying in the dust, his corneas removed. Sly organ thieves no longer come to us as aliens from outer space. Today they may be our next-door neighbors who might just be willing, for some pocket money, to point a finger at fresh and easily accessible kidneys or corneas. Even medical practice is pushing the boundaries outward by extending the life of the rich while cannibalizing the poor—blatant vampirism. For what else can we call the practice of replacing old blood with young blood, as is practiced by wealthy clients at expensive anti-aging clinics.

Popular culture—the new mythological field—helps its consumers digest indigestible reality, to make their peace with it, or accept it, or register it, or help them evade it, so ultimately they can defy it, some in one way, some in another. Popular culture does this in an incomparably more efficient manner than anyone or any other thing. Hannibal Lecter, the protagonist of Thomas Harris's novel—which largely owes its popularity to the brilliant acting of Anthony Hopkins—has lost over the thirty years of the novel's life the profound disgust it used to evoke, and has now acquired an almost romantic caché. The antagonist, Buffalo Bill, obsessed with the idea that human skin is the most perfect fabric for use in sewing apparel, has his artistic "acolytes" today, such as Jessica Harrison, an artist who, in her "Handheld" series, exhibits miniature pieces of furniture that fit in the palm of the hand and look as if they are made from real human skin. "Skin," an art project by Shelley Jackson—who invited participants to have a single (English) word tattooed onto their skin, and, in return, receive a certificate verifying the authenticity of their word—turns Buffalo's dark obsession with human skin into the glorification of the art collective and the mortal work of art.

7.

The lines have blurred, and questions such as "What is art and what is reality?", "What is an imitation of life and what is life?", "What is an imitation of imitation?" have no obvious answers. Yet the most disturbing situation seems to be when our lives come to resemble a cheap horror flick. In January 2014, I watched as such a scene played out on a Zagreb tram. Zagreb is the capital city of Croatia. Croatia was recently granted membership in the European Union, and, as we learned from the *BMC Public Health* journal, is a "burden to Earth." All in all, Croatia is a country with a population of some four million, a half-million of whom are unemployed. The number of the impoverished there is staggering.

A modestly attired, overweight woman, getting on in years, was sitting on the tram. Next to her stood a short man who eyed her with a penetrating, edgy stare.

"So somebody, I see, is living well . . ." said the man in a vaguely general sort of way, and then peered sharply at the woman with a stare that seemed aimed at her through the bore of a revolver.

"Excuse me?" said the woman softly.

"Living well, eh . . . ?" repeated the man louder and more nastily.

"I don't understand what you're saying," repeated the woman, though her facial expression showed she could only guess.

"All I'm saying is that some people sure are living it up . . ." the man would not back down.

The woman bowed her head, as if trying to make herself shrink.

"I weigh 88 pounds, I'm an engineer by training, and I'm unemployed . . ." the man lashed the woman with his words. Clearly he didn't mind if the other tram-goers could hear.

"Is that my fault?! Why not ask for government support . . ." said the beleaguered woman, and stood up to go.

The scene was wrenching. Human flesh weighing 88 pounds was excoriating 200-pound human flesh, certain that 200 pounds of flesh could feel no hunger. And though the woman could have been the resentful man's older sister or even mother, and though the resentful man might swear that such a thing had never crossed his mind, a practiced ear could catch in his protest the wheedle of sexual inadequacy. The woman had clearly upset him, through no fault of her own. She was like a phantom from his deepest subconscious, a banal symbol of his loserdom (fat = rich; thin =

poor). What he longed to do was punch her, wring her neck, make her bleed, bury his teeth in the flesh that weighed twice as much as his, slash the body that was sprawling on the tram seat, indifferent (*"Is that my fault?! Why not ask for government support . . ."*) to his pain.

8.

Many postcommunist, transitional societies have turned their citizens into zombies. In the twenty-first century, "social cohesion and participation" await us, as Willem-Alexander, the Dutch king, has said. "Self-management" as those quick of tongue who follow contemporary trends might call it. "Participation" and "self-management" are actually euphemisms for a scalpel-sharp message: people are being abandoned, today, to their own, bare skin.

An entire team of expert embalmers worked devotedly for years on their masterpiece, their mummy. The most famous mummy of modern times fed and clothed a full team of experts, and for a time it symbolized faith in the idea that a society of equality, brotherhood, and freedom was possible. Today's tattoo parlors—miniature replicas of Lenin's Mausoleum—will, for a mere four hundred euros, suspend their customers in the belief that their tattooed skin is an artwork deserving posterity. Yes, we live in the age of skin. Our age—the corpse we snuggle up next to—is not doing well. Its skin is sallow, purplish stains are surfacing, the skull from which the brain has been removed has cracked open and drawn with it the skin, threatening dark pigment is spreading everywhere, the nails are tinged blue . . . This is exhausting, the embalming is never enough, we daub liquid powder foundation on the postmortem lividity and mask it with our bodies. The stench spreads everywhere, permeating our clothes, hair, lungs, nothing dispels it. Maybe we should throw up our hands and drag the corpse out into the sunlight. Maybe a ray of sunlight will shine upon it and ignite a spark, maybe the corpse will burst into flames all on its own. One thing is certain: fire is a powerful disinfectant.

January 2014

Slow Down!

I'm slowing down the tune,
I never liked it fast.
You want to get there soon,
I want to get there last.

Leonard Cohen, "Slow"

Zagreb, 2013

A late-autumn episode at a Zagreb post office rocked my world.
I have known this post office for some thirty years: three slow-
motion clerks, three windows with protective glass and a hole
through which she, the clerk, and I, the recipient of her ministra-
tions, exchange mutual, silent loathing, the dusty office plants,
the philodendron, ficus, and pothos which will sooner or later
be the death of them, the ladies behind the counter, a green
noose tightening around their necks. The three of them, slow as
Amazonian sloths, type with one finger on their keyboards, lit

by rays of light let in by the narrow window snug up against the ceiling. Their faces show grimaces of suffering and blame, as if some sort of postal mafia chopped off all but the index finger they use to earn their daily bread to warn the post office patrons of what might happen to them if they rebel against the slowness of the service. The general threatening atmosphere is heightened by a pyramid of tidily arranged candles from which flutter blood-colored ribbons with the word "Sale." Why a sale of candles at a post office? I think, and then I remember: All Saint's Day is coming up, when the people of Zagreb converge on the cemetery to genuflect to their dead.

Full of rage at the long, boa-like, undulating line, and relishing the tropical-funereal surroundings, I turn to the young man behind me.

"Did you know that even in Soviet-era Moscow, almost forty years ago, there weren't lines like this? Back then they organized special sales. The thing you wanted to buy would be packaged with something you didn't want or need, but you had to buy them both in order to get what you were after. They called it something like 'buy one, get one that's useless.'"

"I think I'll come back tomorrow," mutters the young man, blanching and fleeing the post office in shock.

I understand. For him I'm a zombie, a being who has risen from the grave and turned up at the post office to frighten him with garbled messages. He has no idea where Moscow is, or what the Soviet Union was, and least of all, any idea what "buy one, get one that's useless" might mean . . . And this, to explain, was the way a customer in the former USSR could purchase products that were in short supply. I remember how during the school year I spent in Moscow I bought a can of Russian salmon with an additional "load" as it was called. For each can of salmon I bought I was forced to purchase useless shoe polish, a tube of inedible tomato paste, a candle, or the like.

In brief, the little post office in the New Zagreb neighborhood of Travno has become for me what the shrine in Međugorje is for Croatian Catholics. I even volunteered to the postal clerks that I'd dust each and every leaf of the philodendrons, the birds of paradise, and the pothos plants with a moist cloth for them, no matter how long it might take.

New York, 1982

When I first came to New York, my friend, a Russian writer and recent émigré who had left the USSR on an "Israeli visa," insisted on taking me around the neighborhood of Brighton Beach. He didn't do this for my sake, but for his own, as I soon realized. I was merely the excuse, his alibi. Brighton Beach was the mirror image of the place he had just fled. He wanted to breathe deep of the simultaneously sobering and intoxicating air of his biosphere, sniff what had been "his," everything he'd run away from. I had said a sentence which pulsated in his mind (*If Odessa is right here in New York, how can you even say you've emigrated?*), and he liked it. At Brighton Beach, in "little Odessa," where mostly Soviet Jews were living at the time, the laws and customs of "Soviet everyday life" had the upper hand. Soviet émigrés waited, and were glad to wait, in long lines out in front of little shops run by fellow Soviet émigrés, thrilled to stand there chatting with their compatriots, just like in the old days, the forever lost Soviet times. These lines in New York's Brighton Beach served as a cushy pillow, a sofa, a couch on which the Soviet émigrés snuggled. The long lines came in handy for socializing, a chance to ease the isolation, rub up against their own, choke back their sudden surge of love for their own kind, while still feeling disgusted by the same. You could purchase Soviet goods in Brighton Beach: jars of pickled vegetables, cans of caviar, dried fish, herring, rye bread, books, records, Russian newspapers . . . The restaurants advertised dance evenings, live music, and Russian singers. Life seemed to be percolating in what were parallel worlds, here in Brighton Beach and there in Manhattan. And my friend, who'd sworn he'd never become like those who waited in line for pickled vegetables, happily settled in on that exact spot, in the niche between the two parallel worlds, so different from one another that time flowed differently in each. In one, faster, in the other, slower? In one forward, in the other back? Nobody could say.

Today, Moscow looks a lot like New York. Meanwhile Zagreb, which is forever boasting that it's a hop, skip, and jump from Vienna, now has the feel of a small Balkan town, though it has sworn that it has never been part of the Balkans and never will be. Several cafés are now gone that brought a lot of pizzazz during the Yugoslav period to the project of imitating Viennese cafés. The poppy seed roll now boldly defends Zagreb's colonial "Austro-Hungarian-ness." Fritters valiantly battle baklava, fried smelt wag their tongues at kebabs, but despite these tasty efforts, Zagreb is slowly sliding into an East European, communist-era urbanity. Or perhaps today, now that Communism is no longer with us, the urbanity of Eastern Europe is more noticeable?

Gerbeaud, the formerly famous Budapest confectionery, which served delicious little goose-liver sandwiches and pastries under Communism that were often finer than the delicacies Vienna is so known for, now serves insipid, watery coffee instead of proper cappuccino, and their Sacher torte is as dry as a cracker. The baffled observer wonders what era they're in, what age they've stumbled into, where, and why have they always thought that time was somehow flowing forward, and not, say, backward, and why did they imagine that it flowed unilinearly anyway, when meandering seems more likely. And then, wonders our observer, is time flowing around and around as if on a Möbius strip? Is time indeed a river into which one cannot step twice?

The Norwegian Revolution

The Norwegian revolution! This was the phrase with which the world media characterized the seven-hour-long live television broadcast of a train ride (the camera was in the engineer's cabin!) from Oslo to Bergen (2009), and a trip two years later from Bergen to Kirkens on board the MS *Nordnorge*. The ship's journey took one hundred thirty-four hours. *Sakte-TV*, the revolutionary Norwegian invention, seems unstoppable. The movie designed to promote Norway was shown at a metro stop in Seoul, and, apparently, was received with accolades. The media discussed slow television, everybody mentioned Warhol and his film *Sleep*, documenting John Giorno's six-hour slumber. The Norwegians also showed *National Firewood Night*, a twelve-hour broadcast of preparations for, the lighting of, and the stoking of a bonfire, and they invited people on Facebook to advise them how best to pile the firewood. Interest was immense.

Just as all began with Marx and Engels in Communism, everything seems to have begun in the "Western world" with Andy Warhol. Yet *Sakte-TV* was modeled not on Andy Warhol, but on Communism. I have seen nothing slower than the weather forecast on Soviet TV. It was usually broadcast just before the television program signed off for the night; I never managed to watch it to the end because I fell asleep, so who knows how late the program actually ran. A soft, sensual, disembodied voice gave the temperatures in Siberia, accompanied by saccharine background music and a slideshow of landscape photographs following one after another so discreetly that where they were from was moot. This was an experience to be remembered. The Soviet Union was vast, there were many rivers, lakes, and cities. The Volga, the Pechora, the Angara, the Ob, the Lena, the Amga, the Aldan, the Irtysh, the Ishim, Lake Ladoga, Lake Baikal, the cities of Magadan, Norilsk, Krasnoyarsk, Omsk, Tomsk, Novosibirsk, Chelyabinsk, Tambov, Penza, Ulan-Ude, Chita, Irkutsk, Angarsk . . .

If, even despite the soporific effect of the weather report, the occasional viewer did not drop off to sleep, the afternoon program was guaranteed to knock them out: a show on preparing cold hors d'oeuvres, without tone or text, filmed in real time. Viewers could watch carrots being sliced into thin rounds and slender sticks, carrots cut into little flowers and a parsley leaf inserted into the very heart of the flower, hard-boiled eggs sliced and little faces made from the eggs with peppercorns, mouths made of thinly sliced onions, and cucumbers, tomatoes, salami, cheese, sausages, onion, mushrooms transformed into elaborate hors d'oeuvres with artistic aplomb. These enchanting marasmatic television shows offered

viewers a feeling of escaping everyday life, or, actually, the feeling that their everyday life was normal, because everyday rivers
not only flow, but freeze over, flood, their water levels change,
as they always have; in everyday life, the cirrus, cumulus, stratus,
and stratocumulus clouds are not only doing their job, but are
denizens of everyday life surrounded by cornucopias from which
little slices of cucumbers, onions, and sausages fly onto plates like
flocks of birds, arranged like rows of little soldiers in rainbow-
colored circles.

**During Communism, there was plenty of time and imagination, and
this may be why it failed**

According to a small news item in *The Guardian* (January 2014),
young scientists Felix Heibeck, Alex Hope, and Julie Legault,
employed at the MIT Media Lab, invented "sensory fiction,"
a kind of "wearable book," consisting of a belt—parachute-like
and worn on the body—and the book itself, connected to the
belt by a cord. Each change in the emotional or physical state
of the protagonist causes discreet changes in the belt, and these
automatically produce changes in the reader's body, accelerating
the pulse, for instance, or altering the body temperature. "Sensory
fiction is a new way of experiencing and creating a story," say the
eager inventors. "Traditional fiction creates and induces feelings
and sympathies through word and image. Connecting the sen-
sors and motivators, the author of sensory fiction acquires new
possibilities for developing the story, mood, and feeling, and then
leaves room for the reader's imagination," claim the inventors of
this "augmented book."

The protagonist of *Nikolai Nikolaevich*, a novella by Yuz Aleshkovsky, is a petty pickpocket, a malingerer and a ne'er-do-well, who has only just been released from prison, but, thanks to his exceptional sexual prowess, finds work at a Soviet institute for scientific research as a sperm donor: a professional masturbator. The scholars impregnate the wives of high-ranking officials, foreigners, and "friends of the Soviet Union," but they secretly plot to send the fertilized ovum rocketing into outer space. Poljenka, a young scientist, uses Nikolai Nikolaevich for her parallel research project. She is interested in which literary texts provide erotic stimulation. She tapes temperature gauges and kinetic electrodes to Nikolai Nikolaevich's penis and brings him various books to read. The young scientist measures how pages of Dostoevsky, Tolstoy, Pushkin, and others act on Nikolai's erection. It turns out that Nikolai Nikolaevich is aroused by a shoemaker's manual from the imperial period, particularly the instructions for how to cobble boots. The satire was written in the 1970s, when it circulated in *samizdat*, and then it was published abroad in Russian, and somewhat later in English, without, unfortunately, much success. Aleshkovsky, who emigrated to the United States in the 1980s, is living out his graying years in Connecticut, a mere hour's drive from MIT, where those earnest scientists came up with "sensory fiction."

People who steal time from God

In his short novel, *Slowness*, Milan Kundera experiences speed as an ecstatic state, but also asks: where has the pleasure in slowness gone, where are the loafing heroes, those who *gaze at God's windows* and bed down under the stars? In the Czech Republic people say of the indolent that they are people who *gaze at God's windows.* In Croatia, such people are said to be *stealing time from God.* A person *gazing at God's windows* is happy, not bored. In our day, indolence is turning into having nothing to do, and this is something quite different. Someone with nothing to do is frustrated, bored, and constantly in search of the activity he lacks, says Kundera.

Kundera's novel was published in 1995, the year taken unofficially as the moment when the internet entered into mass use. Thanks to the readily available plaything, this has meant historical emancipation for a large portion of humanity. The emancipation has been primarily psychological: people have been granted an exhilarating surge of acceleration; a healing sense that they are not *stealing time from God*, but instead are caught up in something deliberate, they feel in control (all this requires is a click of the mouse or the touch of their finger to the screen), and not alone in the world. They're a part of the global community.

Millions of internet users sat before their computer screens— entranced by their grandiose plaything, armed with a do-it-yourself confidence and the magic of transforming unmanageable Earth into something manageable, the size of a Christmas-tree ornament, but meanwhile others, who were spryer, went about actually taking over control and power.

So here we are, a quarter century after the fall of the Berlin Wall. Has this been a lot of time or a little? Have things played out quickly or slowly? To someone who'd slept through the last twenty-five years and woke up only now, the imaginary time stewardess might say: "Welcome to the age of post-democracy!"

In post-democracy we are not stripped of our democratic institutions, not at all, they still exist. Despite the fact that public debate is a "firmly controlled spectacle," run by adversarial teams of those who are experts in "technical persuasion," citizens are able—thanks to the institution of the freedom of choice—to change their governments. Yet most citizens play a "passive, quiescent, even apathetic part," and "behind this spectacle of the election game, politics is really shaped in private by interaction between elected governments and elites which overwhelmingly represent business interests," says Colin Crouch in his text, "Coping with Post-Democracy."

A citizen of the former Soviet Union who refused to work would have had to face the consequences. In post-democracy, *stealing time from God* has been targeted by liberal capitalism as its central bogeyman. Today this phrase is used to stigmatize *leftists, sluggards, anti-capitalists, neo-communists*, no matter where they may be, at demonstrations in Seattle, Paris, London, or New York. *Refugees, migrants* are stealing time from God and have nothing better to do than knock at the doors of rich countries, to be allowed to *laze around on the taxpayers' dime*, of course.

And so we have reached a cynical nexus of today's post-democracy, or at least in its postcommunist version. In the post-Yugoslav states, "transition" served as a euphemism for outright thievery. Anyone—electricians, bankers, truck drivers, murderers, smugglers, confectioners—could get rich overnight by patriotic servicing of the homeland. Croats defended their Croatian homeland (and the desirable part in Bosnia), Serbs defended the Serbian homeland and the Serbian enclaves under threat in Croatia, Bosnia, and Kosovo. Some, while defending the homeland, stole, smuggled, murdered, some did all three, some developed such a taste for it that they killed in vast numbers, some earned "clean money" on the "clean" rhetoric of patriotism. At this moment, the greatest victims of the sudden ascendance of the political and economic elite and their ignorance, arrogance, corruption, and brutality are the hundreds of thousands of people who've been laid off from work, for whom there is no hope they'll ever find other employment, and, with them, the young generation who have not yet found their first job. They are all *leftists*, *sluggards*, *stealing time from God*, *ne'er-do-wells*, *couch potatoes*, or they are simply people who (tsk! tsk!) didn't land on their feet *in time*.

I want more of this stuff

I watched the entire Bergen to Oslo thing after listening to the podcast and I want more of this stuff, commented a viewer who watched the televised train ride. Today, East-European television differs little from the television programs of the West. True, there are more pornographic and unsubstantiated news stories in the East European newspapers, but most often they are owned by the same media corporations, have the same design, and the same array of coverage as those in the West. Thanks to the media, stupidity has now gone global. Replacing relevant articles with irrelevant ones, the media are obliterating cultural memory. Their main task is not so much disinformation, or partial information, as it is the trivialization of information. Consumers of the information at the moment of satiation are hit by the powerful sensation that time has stopped flowing, they are in a timeless hole, dislocated, disconnected, and disoriented. At such a moment we understand the satisfying release felt by the Norwegian train aficionado who was able to forget himself during the hours of watching the train on the Oslo–Bergen line. And we understand our now-extinct Soviet viewer. He reached the same place, not out of a surplus of information and its trivialization, but through lies, isolation, and an information deficit. He, too, at his historical moment, longed to forget himself, and he, too, desired *more of this stuff.*

So what is this about?

What could possibly link the affluent Norwegian, whose future—like the future of his children, his grandchildren, and great grandchildren—is assured because it stands on the solid foundations of vast quantities of petroleum and natural gas, to a communist-era Russian? How did it happen that the two men, the contemporary Norwegian and the extinct Soviet citizen—having come from different times, from different political systems, and different social niches—are faced with the same issues on their TV screen?

Our contemporary Norwegian and our extinct Soviet would seem to have nothing in common. My subconscious is what is connecting them, and the word that links them is revolution, the Norwegian revolution, a phrase I came across in articles about Norwegian slow television. This task was perhaps the work of a semantic paradox, which I didn't notice at first. Slow revolution? Is there anything revolutionary about gazing at God's windows, or gazing at the TV window (television is, after all, a "window onto the world") through which we can watch a seven-hour ride on a train from the perspective of the train's engineer? Can a revolution be slow? Isn't a revolution ecstatically rapid? Modernism has deified speed (the Futurists, Marinetti), and the Russian Revolution fueled the machine of modernism with its best and most efficient fuel. The Russian avant-garde was all about speed, dynamism, thereby flying in the face of the previous artistic period, destroying the old and creating the new. Everything was radically new: language (Khlebnikov, zaum), perspective, oko-literature, art, film, architecture—everything rhymed with the dynamism of the revolution, the new age, the new century, the new ideas, and new technological innovation. The theory of art, the apparatus through which the changes were articulated, it, too, was revolutionary. Stalinism, which began some ten years after the revolution, could be translated, using the vocabulary of speed, as a slamming on of the brakes, a deadlock; in meteorological terms it was a freeze, in medical terms, a coma; in the vocabulary of art it was a throwback to the canon of the nineteenth century (socialist realism). And although the time of Stalinism, as far as I know, was not called a freeze, the period after Stalin's death is known as a thaw.

Do the times of communist autocratism and today's prevailing post-democracy have anything in common? One cannot step into the same river twice, everybody knows that. So, what is this about then? Let's wait until we've lost our patience with the emptiness, the empty democracy, revolutionary TV broadcasts of world marathons in knitting and the stitching of Wiehler needlepoint tapestries. Maybe then we'll know the real answer. If such a thing will even matter at that point, if in the meanwhile we haven't left Earth to move to another planet, if not us, then certainly our avatars, more real and bloodier under the skin than we are.

January 2014

Why We Love Movies About Apes

"I enjoyed the killing . . . it was like going out and stepping on a roach."[4]

An American Vietnam War vet

Dentures

Ratko Mladić is a Serbian general accused of war crimes in Bosnia, the Srebrenica genocide, where some ten thousand Bosnian Muslims were murdered. In late January 2014, Mladić appeared as a witness in the trial of Radovan Karadžić. He availed himself of the opportunity to declare the Hague Tribunal a "Satanic court," to announce "I cannot stand it and do not recognize it." He intimated that he cared less about being acquitted than about what legacy this will leave for his people and his generation. And while all these things sound like the words of someone who was out of control, Mladić's petulant request—"Could the security people bring my teeth from the cells . . ."—when he asked for his

---

4 The British "yellow" press with its strong right-wing bent, as well as some pro-Brexiteers, use the word *roach*, *cockroach* as a demeaning term for migrants.

dentures (so he could speak without mumbling), put things in their proper place.

The ploy with the dentures shows that Mladić is aware not just of his own crimes but of the impact of his behavior. By playing the buffoon, Mladić is doing his level best to undermine the weight of the Srebrenica genocide he is responsible for and flaunt his lack of respect for the institution of the international court. Even in these less than favorable circumstances, Mladić is striving to realize his fantasy of humiliating his opponent. He is the author, director, and actor of the little skit in which he calls for his teeth to be brought; semantically, this was equivalent to passing gas or urinating in front of the judges. It is entirely possible that thanks to the moral and emotional standards of reception held by most media consumers today, Ratko Mladić will be remembered more as a toothless buffoon than as the man who was in charge of the gruesome massacre in Srebrenica. And this is exactly what he is betting on.

This same Mladić, like nearly all of those charged with war crimes, entered a plea of not guilty. One, naturally, has to ask: is there any difference between the buffoonery of Ratko Mladić and that of the democratically chosen political and business elites of Croatia, Serbia, and Bosnia? Granted, the elites are not going around massacring innocent citizens, but they are, in the longer term, cutting off the oxygen. And, meanwhile, members of these elites—happily evading prison sentences—have amassed great wealth thanks to murders, blackmail, wartime and postcommunist malfeasance, plunder and theft; many of them have served in high-level functions (as presidents and prime ministers and from there on down) in governments and elsewhere; indeed, many of them hold these same positions today. When we're talking about justice and guilt, every society has its standards and doesn't appreciate having the standards of others imposed on it.

One of the most malicious "buffoons" of the post-Yugoslav lands is the Serbian radical, Vojislav Šešelj. There are numerous videos of his behavior at the Hague Tribunal, where Šešelj sought dental treatment (he threatened not to testify if he was not allowed access to a dentist), demanded he brought food into the courtroom to show the public how bad the food served to the "jailbirds" was, where he insulted the judges (You are the scum of this world. I'm a [Chetnik] duke, after all!), and where he used vulgar language to undermine the authority of the court.

Radovan Karadžić is also a "buffoon," an "actor," who acted as himself in *Serbian Epics* (1992), an excellent documentary by Paweł Pawlikowski, when he was already in the running as a candidate for future Hague indictee. Karadžić's hiding, his changes of identity, his masks, and the entire screenplay of his arrest prove his directorial, dramaturgical, and thespian artistry. Karadžić is a psychiatrist and a poet (and author of a book with the weird title *Under the Left Breast of the Century*), and the former leader of the Bosnian Serbs. During his many years as a fugitive, Karadžić held a Croatian passport issued to one Petar Glumac (the word *glumac* means actor!), with which he was captured in Austria, but then released. Somewhat later he was arrested again and finally handed over to the Hague Tribunal, but now under yet a third identity, as Dr. Dragan David Dabić, an alternative healer, a self-designed Gandalf. All three of him are now in the Hague prison.

The entire history of the collapse of Yugoslavia might be treated as Theater of Cruelty; it hasn't been dropped from the repertoire for a quarter century; a stage on which, evening after evening, acts of "buffoonery" are played, which send chills down your spine. Ron Haviv's war photographs are iconic. One of his pictures shows Željko Ražnatović Arkan, a master at theatricalizing his life as a criminal. Behind him stand his cutthroats, the *Tigers* paramilitary group, armed to the teeth, and there in front of them stands Arkan, holding a live tiger cub by the scruff of its neck. Another photograph shows two Serbian murderers in Vukovar. One of them sports a bushy "Chetnik" beard and a typical Chetnik fur hat, while the second is younger and more striking, in a quirky costume, looking like Alex from *A Clockwork Orange*: a top hat on his head and a fox-fur pelt flung around his neck. All of us have been in the audience of this theater for a quarter century, we are witnesses but also participants in the theatricalization of crime, the refusal to admit guilt, the birthing of new national "heroes." We have managed to convince ourselves that the curtain has dropped, the ghastly performance is done, the theater shuttered, and we went home ages ago. But then the new episodes come along: Mladić's dentures, or the recent heartfelt homecoming for Dario Kordić, a Croatian murderer of Bosnian Muslims, who returned after serving out his Hague sentence, or the national euphoria when Ante Gotovina was acquitted—and they remind us that the show is still on, the actors still alive, and, moreover, they have scads of loyal admirers and fans; there is no end in sight.

And most awful of all, every one of us, as is true of every steady-going, enduring sadomasochistic relationship, has become inured to the daily dose of humiliation. We've lost our voice, words, sight, hearing, and reason in the process; we've dehumanized ourselves. For we, too, the audience, we have "theatricalized," we recognize each other only barely as at a play being put on somewhere else, in a distant realm where people speak another language. Hey, aren't they us, we ask, and then, yet again, we forget.

The Act of Killing

Murderer Anwar Congo is the protagonist of the documentary film *The Act of Killing* (by authors Joshua Oppenheimer, Christine Cynn, and an anonymous Indonesian, 2012). And he, just like Ratko Mladić, has a thing about his teeth. Perhaps his narcissistic fixation on his dentures, putting them in and taking them out throughout the movie, makes him seem more human. Or perhaps the opposite is true. This detail may, in fact, be a small directorial manipulation intended to shock the moviegoers into awareness. At one moment viewers may feel sickened by how readily they have become desensitized to the sea of blood, yet are still disgusted by Congo's dentures.

The Act of Killing is a masterpiece. Many will come away misremembering the title as *The Art of Killing*, and they will not be far wrong, because the director's strategy is all about rankling the viewer's deadened sensitivities. He gives Anwar Congo, a murderer, a free hand to make the movie about himself and his crimes. Most of it consists of the amateur theatricalization of the crimes from the murderer's viewpoint. The executions went on in Indonesia in the mid-seventies, during Suharto's time in office. These were massive anti-communist purges; as many as three million people may have been killed. Anwar Congo boasts that he, personally, killed a thousand. Most of the executions were done "gangster-style." Indeed, the paramilitaries call themselves *preman*—meaning "free man"—but also "gangster." The executions went hand in hand with robbery. The executioners first robbed the "communist" victims, and then killed them. The precise number of people killed has never been substantiated, and nobody has ever called the murderers to account. Today's rightwing paramilitary organization, the Pemuda Pancasila, grew out of these anti-communist death squads. The organization is estimated to number over three million members, who see their task as being "servants of the nation," to fight neo-communists and leftists. Jusuf Kalla, vice president of Indonesia at the time the movie was made, says, in a speech to the gangsters: "This nation needs free men . . . We need our gangsters to get things done!"

Aside from Anwar Congo, we meet an array of other murderers in the movie. The murderers, we learn, were not a lone band, but a parallel hand of the regime. Many took part in the work of killing, such as Ibrahim Sinik, the owner of a newspaper, who put together lists of potential victims. ("Why would *I* do such grunt work?! One wink from me and they're dead!") Some did the killing so they could afford fancy clothes and have spending money, others killed to get rich and go into "business," and yet others did so in order to move into political positions and take hold of power. One of the murderers, Adi Zulkadry, Congo's friend, agreed to act in Congo's psychodrama. He tells his buddy, Anwar, that killing is the worst thing you can do . . . and you must come up with an excuse for your actions so you can live with yourself afterward. Money can be an acceptable excuse, and besides, the question of morals is "relative" anyway, says Adi. In response to questions asked by journalists about the crimes he committed, Adi says, "War crimes are defined by the winners. I'm a winner, so I can make my own definition. I have no need to be guided by international definitions. And what's most important, all that is truthful is not necessarily good. We shoved wood in their anuses until they died. We broke their necks. We hanged them. We strangled them with wire. We cut off their heads. We ran them over with cars. We were allowed to. And the proof is, we murdered people and were never punished. [. . .] I have never felt guilty, never been depressed, never had nightmares."

There is a scene in the movie where Anwar Congo forces his grandsons, two boys, to watch a scene he filmed earlier. Anwar chooses a scene in which, for a change, he is not acting the executioner, but the victim. The other amateur actors interrogate him and feign a brutal beating . . . "This is your grandfather!" Congo says to his grandsons, genuinely touched by his own position as victim in the scene.

Jihadists prefer Nutella

If you allow yourself to be bombarded by images—as I did in the summer of 2014—the images in *Serbian Epics* (1992), in *The Act of Killing* (2012), and the images of jihadists and ISIS that were circulating online, you may come away as I did feeling there is no difference among killers. I also admit that I don't see the differences because I am a woman. All the murderers are men.

Regardless of age, race, faith, geography, and self-determination, all the murderers publicly declare their reverence for God (some even see themselves as God's emissaries, such as the jihadists) and their leaders. The ISIS–jihadists love Allah and their caliph, Abu Bakr al-Baghdadi. The world of murderers is a man's world that invokes its God. The *Serbian Epics* documentary makes the point perfectly about male fraternity punctuated with ritual lamps, priests, the licking of the altar, invocations of a glorious (fabricated!) warrior past, praise for traditional values, and baptisms for the unbaptized. All these murderers seek spiritual justification for their future crimes: all of them kill for God and in the name of God, for their people and in the name of their people. "God hates the communists," says an Indonesian right-wing political figure in his speech to young gangsters. Each murderer's equipment consists of a knife and a modest packet of ideology.

The world of murderers is a world without women (they are an absent object of hatred and disrespect). It is a world of male intimacy and the passing-on of experience and knowledge from "fathers" to "sons." In the documentary footage playing before me, I am following scenes of ease and relaxation among Serbian soldiers, scenes expressing mutual loyalty and intimacy among Indonesian murderers (massages, group singing and socializing, intimate conversations), and scenes of physical intimacy when the jihadists swim together in the Tigris.

Murderers love themselves most of all, and this self-love knows no bounds. "Stupidity is in love with itself and its self-love is boundless," says Croatian writer Miroslav Krleža. Therein lies the resilience of stupidity. In self-love lies the resilience of murderers. Anwar Congo says this was a time "when we were killing happily." An Indonesian "gangster" summarizes the point of the killing in two words: "Relax and Rolex." In other words, the killing brings with it both satisfaction and financial gain: Keep calm and carry on.

Murderers have cell phones. This refers specifically to jihadists, not because they are more attached to technology than Ratko Mladić, but because technology developed in the interim. Murderers today can be recognized by the way they're always in the company of other men, they deck themselves out with weapons— and cell phones. Their cell phones are less for communication, more for access to the Internet, where they post their selfies, armed with Kalashnikovs and Nutella (jihadists adore Nutella!), photographs in which they are surrounded by the heads they have lopped off, videos of iron gates on which still more decapitated heads are impaled, photographs of victims crucified on crosses. Thanks to technology, we have evidence, public and accessible to all, of the crimes these murderers committed. Technological innovation and self-love go hand in hand. For the visual "content" generously offered by the murderers, there is a broad and remarkably receptive public, which itself produces millions of selfies and sends them from all geographical corners of the world. There are kids who send selfies they take with homeless people they've just beaten up on the streets of their cities, or with little girls they've just molested. There are kids who send breezy school-trip selfies from Auschwitz. They are all of them directors in the miniature Theater of Cruelty, all busily theatricalizing their everyday life.

The theatricalization of evil grows ever richer and more effective. One of the first productions of this type to arrive from the newly founded Islamic state was the video with American journalist

James Foley. Foley was dressed in an orange jumpsuit; next to him stood a jihadist in black, holding a knife. First Foley read a text, addressing his family and the United States, and then the jihadist stepped forward. Within seconds, Foley was beheaded. The jihadist Theater of Cruelty would soon acquire more skilled directors, stage-set designers, and costume designers. Under the heavens there is nothing shameless. God loves a good show.

Anwar Congo is particularly proud of a scene of absolution from sin, where a waterfall symbolically rinses away all the blood and guilt, lithesome Indonesian women dance alluringly, while a victim drapes a gold medal around Anwar's neck and says, "For executing me and sending me to heaven, I thank you a thousand times." Congo is visibly moved by his own creation: "I never imagined I could possibly create something so immense. Because of one thing I am truly proud, and that is how the waterfall expresses such deep emotions." Oh right, and that all murderers care deeply about emotions.

Thank you

From start to finish I have followed the war in ex-Yugoslavia and its aftermath—still ongoing—and for me, when I compare my own years of experience with these two other randomly chosen experiences on film (there were dozens and dozens of others I could have chosen among, from World War II to today), the words that the hapless extra delivers while draping the big gold medal around Congo's neck sound completely normal to me: "For executing me and sending me to heaven, I thank you a thousand times." At least to my ear, this sounds like the only normal line in the documentary. So I find it easy to carry on in the same vein . . . For executing me and sending me to heaven, I thank you a thousand times, because if you hadn't, I would have had to go on seeing your contorted snouts, which have populated all regions and landscapes, regardless of where; your snouts are all the same, your species is invasive, you are as indestructible as ragweed, your mentality is always the same, as if all of you spring from the same genetics factory. Thank you for the thousandth time that you killed me and sent me to heaven, because otherwise I'd have had to watch your faces leaking from everywhere, TV screens, newspapers, bookstore displays. You have occupied every millimeter of public space, you are as tenacious as superweeds, there is no way, no way whatsoever, to uproot you, you have slithered into every pore of life, our nostrils, the air we breathe, the water we drink . . . So thank you for beheading me and sending me to heaven, because if you hadn't, I might have borne children: a boy who'd grow up to be a murderer like you, and a girl you'd rape one day and then subject to your male standards, yes, you, your sons, or the like. So thank you for dispatching me to heaven, because otherwise I would have had to go on reading reports about what you're reading this summer, where you're vacationing, what sort of yacht you sail, what you think about this or that, your strategy for addressing problems, otherwise I'd have had to see what your estates look like in the magazines or on my computer screen, your private zoos, the animals you've stuffed and mounted, the decapitated deer head that watches you from the wall of your weekend getaway, everywhere, in the Sumatran jungle, on the rolling verdant hillsides of Croatia and Serbia, in the Iraqi oil fields . . . So thanks for blowing my head off and sending me to heaven, because if you hadn't, I'd have to see your art collections, your wealth dripping blood, I'd have to read your memoirs, which you leave to your offspring so they'll remember you, stumble everywhere over your legacy for your people and your generation, because this is what concerns you most, because of this legacy you don't pick and choose the means, you'll find a way by hook or by crook to elbow into a place in history, damn you, history . . . Thank you for stabbing me with your knife and sending me to heaven, because if you hadn't I'd still be forced to look at the slimy horizons intersected by your tentacles, for you are a mega-octopus, your resilience is in your appendages: when one is chopped off, another grows. Thank you for killing me and sending me to heaven, because if you hadn't, every day I would have had to face not only the banality of your evil (that part will be easy!), but your appalling vitality.

Ape not kill ape

When nothing else helps, when the brain grinds to a halt, when you give up on banging your head against the wall of the same tedious question for which there never is an answer (How could it be, and how can it be possible, that this is all repeating itself in ever shorter intervals?), then that same brain, like a dry sponge, sops up answers where it can. Maybe herein lies some of the enchanting appeal of ape movies for millions of viewers. Many sorts of enchantment come and go, but the human fascination with apes endures.

The psychologically most intriguing detail (to which my friends attest) seems to be that the word *ape* (humanoidea, tailless simians, most human-like) is experienced by many as male. Although in our imaginary there are images of female apes nursing, cuddling, stroking their young, the word "ape" is strongly marked by gender. The ape in our human imaginary is always male! Perhaps for this reason the themes of the organizations of ape communities, defense, rivalry, battle, and leadership pertain only to males. And perhaps because the females are preoccupied with other concerns, they are invisible in the male world.

Apes are our (male!) mirror image, our archetypal self. We are fascinated by them not only because *they* are similar to *us*, but because *we* are similar to *them*. They are our cathartic mirror, this is why we love them, they are the answer to the questions we seek while banging our head on the ungiving wall.

If someone were to run a research project asking men to choose their favorite (female) star in the world of science of today, I am sure the brilliant anthropologist Jane Goodall would win. Even men who have no clue as to what anthropology is would vote for her. Why? Because Jane Goodall doesn't work only with apes, but also with that large hairy animal with a mournful gaze, which lies dormant in every man. Jane, whether she wants to be so or not, is every man's dream girl: she is Tarzan's Jane, she is also Ann Darrow, the petite human female who looks as if she fell out of a Kinder Surprise egg, and she still doesn't realize she is the lethal bullet that will bring King Kong down in the end. She, on her part, understands his wild and deeply emotional nature, and she knows that his "wildness" is natural, sincere, and unblemished.

The most recent sequel of the ape saga, *Dawn of the Planet of the Apes*, is crisscrossed with meanings like every fairy tale.

Every detail of the movie entices us to an ideological reading, starting with the name Koba: a species of African ape, but also Niokolo-Koba—the Senegalese national park, and even Stalin's nickname (!). Koba's lines, such as, "Humans! You ape prisoner now! You will know life in cage!" elicit howls of delight in movie theaters worldwide. Understanding that Koba will destroy people and apes and that he needs to be confronted and conquered, for "ape always seek strongest branch," Caesar, the "reasonable" ape, overcomes "unruly" Koba. (Another detail, this one dental, warrants mention: Koba is recognizable, among the other apes, for his prominent canines, his teeth!)

"Ape not kill ape," says Koba, once he is subdued, trying with his last flash of cunning to bribe Caesar and remind him of his (Caesar's) program, by which he had homogenized and emancipated the ape community. After a long silence, when the viewers' hearts are in their mouths, when they are already fearing Caesar will take his ape brother's side, Caesar utters Koba's death sentence: "You are not ape."

August 2014

Long Live Work!

Factories demand

Workers must command

Primer, 1957

1.

A Bulgarian grocery store opened for business in my Amsterdam neighborhood. On the inside of the plate-glass window they hung a Bulgarian flag, making the store highly visible from the outside, but dark inside. They sell overpriced Bulgarian groceries. And the same can be said of almost all the ethnic markets. First come the migrants, and after them—the markets. After a time the ethnic food markets disappear, but the migrants? Do they stick around? The number of Bulgarians in the Netherlands is clearly on the rise; two Bulgarian markets have opened recently in my neighborhood alone. And as to those with a "Balkan tooth," they have famously deep pockets as far as food is concerned; they'll happily shell out a euro or two extra to satisfy gourmandish nostalgia. The markets sell Bulgarian wine, frozen kebapcheta 000 and meat patties, cheese pastries (*banitsas*), pickled peppers and cucumbers, kyopolou, pindjur, lyutenitsa, and sweets that look as if they've come from a package for aid to the malnourished: they are all beyond their shelf dates. The store is poorly tended and a mess, customers are always tripping over cardboard boxes. Next to the cash register sits a young man who doesn't budge, more dead than alive, it's as if he has sworn on his patron saint that nobody will ever extract a word from him. The young woman at the cash register is teen-magazine cute. She has a short skirt, long straight blond hair, a good tan. Her tan comes from her liquid foundation; her cunning radiates like the liquid powder. She files her nails, and next to her stands a small bottle of bright red nail polish. The scene fills me with joy. She grins slyly. I buy *lyutenitsa*, Bulgarian (Turkish, Greek, Macedonian, Serbian) cheese, and three large-size Bulgarian tomatoes. *Dovizhdane. Довиждане.*

I know that every European right-wing heart warms to this description. True, the "Easterners," the Bulgarians, Romanians, Poles, not only steal, drink, and lie, but they bring with them their own pickles, *their own* swill. They can hardly wait to milk our welfare system, move into our subsidized housing, which they then sublet to others while they go back to their houses and lounge and laze around with the money they've ripped off from us taxpayers. Of course the Bulgarians, Romanians and Poles think the same of *their* Roma; and until recently the Bulgarians thought likewise of *their* Turks. Ever since educated Bulgarian women have been rushing off to Turkey in droves, however, to earn a little pocket money as housekeepers, the constellation of products and the erosion of stereotypes has shifted to the advantage of the Turks.

2.

The division into those who work and those who do not—the hardworking and the indolent, the diligent and the ne'er-do-wells, the earnest and the couch potatoes—is hardly new, but over the last few years it has become the basic media-ideological matrix around which revolve the freethinkers of the general public. Joining the category of the indolent, ne'er-do-wells, and malingerers are the ranks of the jobless (for whom the employed claim they are simply incompetents and bumblers), along with the grumblers, indignants, and the groups defined by their country, geography, and ethnicity (Greeks, Spaniards, Romanians, Bulgarians, Serbs, Bosnians—all shiftless riffraff!), anti-capitalistic elements, hooligans, vandals, terrorists, and Islamic fundamentalists.

In response to the question of how to become a multimillionaire, one of the wealthiest Russian oligarchs replied: "Don't you forget, I work seventeen hours a day!" The very same answer is given by criminals, thieves, politicians, porn stars, war profiteers, celebs, mass murderers, and other similar deplorables. They all say *seventeen hours a day*, *my career*, and *my job* with such brash confidence, not a twitch to be seen. On *Meet the Russians*, a TV show broadcast by Fox, young, prosperous Russians, many of them born, themselves, into money, fashion models, fashion and entertainment industry moguls, pop stars, club owners, and the like, all use the following phrases: *I deserve this; everything I have, I've earned; my time is money; I work 24/7; I never give up.*

The media (they, too, work 24/7!) have managed to persuade the nonworking majority that this is so. And while the *lazy* majority has no career, or profession, or first and last name, or even a face, the faces of the *hardworking* minority are with us twenty-four hours a day. As far as women go, of course, the ass often replaces the face. The ass has its (ethnic) identity, and a first and last name (*Guess whose gorgeous ass this is?*—is a regular headline in Croatian newspapers). And meanwhile the ne'er-do-wells have become Earth's burden, they slow its rotation, nobody knows how to jettison them, and they'd be best off taking matters into their own hands. This is why the Singapore movie *Ilo Ilo*, directed by Anthony Chen, begins with the unambiguous fall of an anonymous body from the balcony of a Singapore apartment building. The movie speaks about the impact of the Asian financial crisis on the "indolent": they turn to drink, plunge from their balconies, kill themselves.

3.

Short news items, such as a report from Rexecode, the Parisian center for monitoring macroeconomic development, sometimes snatch a little column space in the media in places like Croatia and Serbia, tucked in between the bigger headlines such as: "You won't believe the gorgeous asses vacationing this summer on the Adriatic beaches." The results shown by the Rexecode research project on the hours people work in Europe show that the *lazy* Romanians are the absolute record-holders in terms of the number of hours they spend on the job. The *lazy* Greeks come in second, and the *lazy* Bulgarians, third. After them come the Croats, Poles, Latvians, Slovaks, Estonians, and Cypriots. Working the least are the *diligent* Finns, while the legendarily *industrious* Germans are somewhere mid-scale. Such news flashes do little, regrettably, to uproot the deep-seated prejudices, in fact they reinforce them. The *diligent* have won the day, not only in real terms, but symbolically as well. The *indolents* are despised by all, and most of all by the indolents themselves. They themselves look up to, even deify, the hard-workers (meaning: the superrich). The news that there are no more than two hundred *hard-workers* in little Croatia, while everybody else is *indolent* (whether jobless or working, they are all equally hungry) has prompted Croatian legislators to propose a new labor law, with the blessings of the *hard-workers*; the new law apparently strips the *indolents* of all rights, except the right to the barest of existences.

4.

The native armed with bow and arrow, railway line, village, town, may the country thrive and grow, long live, long live work. These are the lyrics of a song that was sung during the Socialist period, when workers' rights were much greater than they are today. I confess I never made sense of these verses, perhaps because I didn't try. What possible connection could there be between a native armed with bow and arrow and railway lines, villages, and towns, unless the lyrics are an anticipatory tweet about the eons of history of the human race: in other words, thanks to the appeal of hard work, natives traded in their bows and arrows for railways, villages, and towns. Or, perhaps, it's the other way around: without the redeeming balm of work, those same natives would have to return to the age of bows and arrows, while weeds would engulf the railway lines, villages and towns. Although the everyday life of socialism in ex-Yugoslavia was like a hedonistic parody of the everyday life in other communist countries, Yugoslavs shared with them a packet of the same values, a set of common symbols, and their imaginary. And at the center, at least as far as symbols and the imaginary go, was work. Work was what persuaded the native armed with bow and arrow to evolve from the ape, and the "peasant and worker" and "honest intellectuals" evolved thereafter from the native. "The workers, peasants, and honest intellectuals" were the pillars, in the socialist imaginary, of a robust socialist society and were cast in a powerful positive light, especially because the *honest* intellectuals were separated from *dishonest* intellectuals just as the wheat is winnowed from the chaff. The "bureaucracy" was the necessary evil, the "bureaucracy" flourished, while feeding, parasite-like, on the people. In any case, the word "work" was heard everywhere: in the news shorts that played before films in Yugoslav movie theaters, in the images of eye-catching, sweaty, workers' muscles, in my elementary school primers where the occupations were unambiguous (male miners, female nurses, male blacksmiths, female backhoe-operators, male construction workers, female teachers, male engineers, female tram-drivers), in the movies, and in the First-of-May parades—pagan-like rites, honoring the god of labor as tons of sacrificial steel, coal, wheat, books were rolled out. The heroes of the day were the record-breakers, the men and women who went above and beyond the norm. The heroes of today are pop stars, Marko Perković Thompson and Severina, and the many clowns who surround them.

5.

Today the vistas I see are post-Yugoslav. Perhaps the view is better in the postcommunist countries like Poland, Romania, Bulgaria, Hungary . . . I hope representatives of other postcommunist countries don't hold against me my geopolitically narrow focus. Everything I've said refers only to little Croatia, little Serbia, little Bosnia, little Macedonia . . . And this crumb of badness in the sea of postcommunist goodness can easily be ignored, can it not? Although to be honest, research from 2007 shows that fewer than half of the Germans living in what used to be East Germany were pleased with the current market economy, and nearly half of them desired a return to socialism. As a return to the previous order is now unimaginable, the *lethargic* East German grumblers have been given a consolation prize, a little nostalgic souvenir, a MasterCard and on it the face of Karl Marx, designed and issued by a bank in the city known today as Chemnitz, though earlier it was called Karl-Marx-Stadt.

6.

The Russian oligarch, who said: "Don't forget, I work seventeen hours a day!" seems to have forgotten a lesson he'd imbibed in his earliest years. In Russian fairy tales, Ivan the Simple earns his happy ending and wins the kingdom and the queen. Does he do this by working seventeen hours a day? No he does not. He does this thanks to his cunning and his powerful helpers: a horse able to traverse miles and miles at lightning speed, a magic shirt that makes him invincible, a fish that grants his wishes, Baba

Yaga who gives him sly advice, and powerful hawks and falcons for brothers-in-law. Even our hero—Ivanushka, grimy, ugly, slobbering Ivanushka Zapechny, he who is the least acceptable, who lounges all the livelong day by the tile stove—even he, such as he is, wins the kingdom and the princess without breaking a sweat. Our modern fairy tale about the seventeen-hour workday has been cooked up as consolation for the losers. Who are the majority, of course.

The young woman at the cash register in the Bulgarian market knows all this; she files her nails and waits for one of the *hard-workers* who will turn her from a frog into a princess. Her seventeen-hour workday at the cash register at a neglected ethnic grocery in Amsterdam will not deliver her the transformation she's hoping for.

In the movie *This Must Be the Place*, Sean Penn plays the role of a rich, aging rock star who says: "Have you noticed how nobody works anymore and everybody does something artistic?"

July 2014

Don't Take It Personally

"They ate, they drank, behind they left nothing for us."

Roma fairy tale

The Slovenian pop group *Zaklonišče prepeva* [Air-Raid Shelter Singing] recorded the song "Samo da prođe demokratija" ["If Only Democracy Would Pass"]. Their video made the rounds in the post-Yugoslav countries on the internet and in social media when it came out in 2014. There have been several other videos like it over the last twenty years. The band wasn't particularly compelled by originality, in fact not at all. Using trite language and images, they assault our flagging, benumbed memory. Everything in the video—the music, the words, the backdrop—is a belabored quotation. The empty industrial hall, the actors there as extras, the band striking poses straight off of old communist posters, their gazes suggesting an unwavering faith in the future, the singer with his Che Guevara beret. There's an accordion player

with an accordion, and three flags—blue, white, red—symboliz-
ing the Yugoslav divorce, while the red star, of course, is nowhere
to be seen. Everything in the video has an amateurish feel, and
the lyrics are squeamishly thick with clichés.

*I've come down from horse to mule, I plod along like a ragtag fool, no
longer do I buy the fairy tales / I slave at two, three jobs a day, never an
end to the bills to pay, how do old mothers ever survive / Our grand-
fathers fought in the war, many of them gave their lives, is this what
we were fighting for? / They sent Krauts and King packing, they knew
he was a hack, they toppled every single foe / If only democracy would
pass, and straight to hell with the top dogs, dogs / If only democracy
would pass, so we can live again like people. / The top dogs rake in the
dough, play golf, drive Jaguars, on our backs sit the scum / There is only
a handful of them but a whole pack of us, losers, let's show them they
are done.*

While listening to the lead singer's clarion voice, the older listener
can't believe that someone so young would be revisiting the spent
language of social critique—the language of the 1970s student
demonstrations, the peasant uprisings against greedy landown-
ers and cruel tax collectors, the language of political criticism
with a vocabulary that was central to the Partisan movement
(their great-grandfathers!) (*foes, Krauts, top dogs,* etc.). Yet this
pop-protest is aimed at the current transition phases that are still
ongoing (although the Yugoslav divorce happened some twenty
years ago!). One might easily misread the last line, "let's show
them they are done" as: "let's show them we are done." The most
visually and semantically striking detail in the video is at the end:
the inflatable Father Frost on the floor of the empty hall, deflated

and trampled. The camera lingers on Father Frost as he gradually inflates and fills out. The video attracts post-Yugoslavs; its appeal lies in its precision, stripped of all affect, and its feel for the hopelessness of protest inherent in the very call to protest.

So here we are, we've broken through to the end, we've reached democracy's nadir. The more protests there are, the less effective they become; the more channels there are for sending messages, the less the messages are heard. We are all denizens of Hyde Park, each of us with our right to the speaker's corner. Political language has lost the impact of faith and conviction, it is emptied of meaning: people organize themselves by herd instinct, to the left and to the right, believing that thanks to the *left wing* or to the *right wing* they'll keep their job, or find a job, or, maybe, retire. The language of political protest has lost its muscle, protesters come and go. Slogans, nudity, flowers in hair, women's bared breasts, the living Jesus on the cross, self-immolation, the Hong Kong umbrellas—all of these flash through the papers and across screens and quickly sink away into darkness.

Maybe we should have listened, twenty years ago, to what the peasant women at the outdoor market were saying. The newly ensconced Croatian authorities in the early 1990s introduced many changes, among these a brief disruption to the daily life of Dolac—Zagreb's central outdoor food market—by sending armed guards in special uniforms to patrol the marketplace. The peasants who came to the market to sell their wares—women from the villages near Zagreb, selling homemade cottage cheese, corn bread, and fresh eggs—did not appreciate the presence of the uniformed guards. When the boys in blue showed up, the women signaled to one another, "Girls, watch out, democracy is coming, time to go!"

More than twenty years have passed between the line "Girls, watch out, democracy is coming, time to go!" and the lyric "If only democracy would pass, so we can live again like people." Twenty-five years have passed since the Berlin Wall came down. Will anyone, amid the euphoria of the celebrations, have the presence of mind to ask what has happened, lo these many years? Why would young people today be hoping for "democracy" to disappear so they could "live again like people"?!

Why does an old woman in Sarajevo light a candle for Tito every year on the anniversary of his death? It's because she believes Tito emancipated women in Yugoslavia by allowing them to stop wearing the hijab. Today, the old woman's great-granddaughter is back to wearing a hijab and disapproves of her great-grandmother's "emancipated past."

The institution of the church, which has drawn women back under its wing, is doing a bang-up job of subjugation, and has made itself the closest ally of the post-Yugoslav "democratorships," the new states—busy producing a simulacrum of democracy. As an institution, the church is more efficient than the state: there are more hours in schools of catechism class than there are of computer science; there are more crosses on the walls of Croatian hospitals than there are supplies of hypodermics, bandages, and cotton batting. The hospitals suffer from a shortage of nurses, but not from a shortage of priests and nuns poised to hold vigil by the bedsides of the dying; thanks to the church's pro-life propaganda, a fifth public hospital in Croatia has now decided to deny abortion services. The church is the most totalitarian and efficient system of all: they take everything, and in return they sell the tepid water of consolation.

What are the democratic options available to retirees? Retirees cannot cover basic costs with their pensions, or, if they can, they end up supporting their unemployed children. What democratic options are available to Croats, Serbs, Bosnians, Macedonians, and others, who have found themselves out of work in their fifties? Or what about the youngsters graduating from schools and universities every year and starting their professional lives? What democratic freedoms are available to the vast majority of people who do not have the resources to pay for attorneys, dentists, doctors, to school their children, or even to afford a roof over their heads? Democracy today is an umbrella term that encompasses many things: the praxis of merciless capitalist exploitation, the unfree media, media manipulation, the censorship of corporate capitalism, the production of lies, modern slavery . . . Meanwhile there are groups like a group in Split, calling itself the "Urban Right-Wing," who use their democratic right to protest by putting up posters everywhere with the words: *Death to Communism!* Where is the Communism whose death they're demanding? Where's it hiding? In the salesrooms of Croatian IKEA?

There aren't many animal species on Earth that devour their own kind. Rats, in this regard, are the masters: if they lose a food source, they eat their closest kin. So do people. If you've recently experienced people jostling you on the sidewalk, or snarling something nasty at you; or if someone walking by yanks the gold chain off your neck, or if people who used to be friends and acquaintances stop answering your emails; or if you can no longer count on the promises you're given: the promise of the carpenter who said he'd come to repair your window, the promise of the gas man and the plumber, the promise of your hairdresser and pedicurist, anybody's promise. If your neighbor's ten-year-old kid spat in your face while the two of you were taking the elevator, don't worry, this is no figment of your imagination, yes, it's really happening, you aren't paranoid, the ten-year-old kid did spit in your face. But don't take it to heart. Don't take it personally. Because all this isn't happening just to you, it's happening to everyone, people have trouble talking about it, the humiliation is far too widespread, so why acknowledge the little slights, though, to be frank, they're the ones that hurt the most. No, things are not yet horrible, telephones still work, your best friends have you over on Saturday to celebrate a birthday, the messages from your acquaintances still appear in your email, though it's true that there aren't as many as there used to be. They appear, when you provide the initiative, you exchange the requisite messages, and then you and the other side sink again into many months of silence, after which the feeble bell rings once more, only to go quiet forever . . . Don't take it personally, we're at war, we have begun to annihilate each other, our supply of food and dignity have been cut off, we're useless. No, it's not that people are being worse to you in particular, this applies to everyone, and they just happened to stumble across you, and the crueler they are, the more unfriendly—the greater their own anxiety. If you think you're sinking, don't take it personally, the people who are preventing you from clinging to the life raft are only on it themselves briefly, because they are better at shoving away the wretches who are drowning, including you. But I tell you, don't worry, soon enough they, too, will find themselves in the cold, dank water, someone else will push them overboard soon enough, unless they're kept on board to serve as food.

So pay close attention, you've watched your share of Mad Maxes, you know what you need to do. The war is upon us, stock up your cellars, stow away some extra gasoline, you never know, a supply of matches and candles, shelves of canned food—these will come in handy when you need to trade, and you'll keep yourself going with cunning. I tell you, the war is on, class against class, everyone against everyone, individuals against individuals, the signals still may be a challenge to decipher, but the war is here. Didn't your next-door neighbor elbow you in the ribs just yesterday in passing? Crazy, you thought, as you weighed whether to confront them. Soon you'll have to, because there will be no other option, you'll barricade yourself in, drag home sandbags, we're at war, it's just that we haven't quite faced this yet, perhaps because we were on the lookout for clear signs of the apocalypse, but there is no apocalypse, only the post-apocalypse; this apocalypse is like diabetes, you don't even know when you have it. Brace yourselves, because soon you'll have to confront the faces of those who used to be on your side: the illiterate, brutal, armed to the teeth, the raging, wild, hungry, yes, the cannibals, the people who stayed alive themselves by relying on one skill alone—the skill of survival. And if you make it through this, if we make it through this, then maybe one day we'll live again like people.

October 2014

Good Morning, Losers!

Who fails to learn when wet behind the ears,
Will have trouble in their later years.

Primer, 1957

1.

"I'd like to interview Jenn J.," a friend from my ex-country, who is now living in Sweden, writes to me in an email.

"Who?" I ask.

Jenn J. is the proprietor of a small shop selling cloth gift bags, sacks, and pouches. She lives on the Upper West Side in New York with her husband, three lovely daughters, and her cat, Pongo. Her website offers a glimpse of her life, which looks like an ad for happiness. Jenn J. is a svelte blond, a northern European type, her husband is tall, strong, and also a northerner, their daughters are pretty, blond teenagers, sylphlike creatures. A wooden cottage in the northern climes is a dream we all share, with a stately tree mid-lawn, little girls blinking sleepily from a hammock, the sun dappling the grass, the family romping—it shows us that happiness does exist. And their four-story house in New York is a dream come true. The spot was chosen by Jenn J., who has known since childhood that New York is her city. She has always cared deeply about ecology, and, as a stylist by trade, she thought long and hard about what she could personally do to make the world a better place. When she tallied up how many trees sacrifice their lives for the paper she was using to wrap her Christmas presents, Jenn J. realized that salvation for Earth lay in cloth gift bags. So she designed little bags, *organizer* sacks and pouches for us to use when storing our shoes, blow-dryers, sneakers, jewelry, cosmetics, medicine, socks, computer cables—everything that can be kept in a sack, that doesn't require a larger container. She designed sacks with large monogrammed letters, pouches in an array of colors and designs, bags for kids, gift bags for wrapping Christmas presents. Jenn J. has conjured for us a paradise of bags. The bags offer us a feeling that, together with our things, we'll stow away in them all our troubles and fears, our faults and our worries, and we'll finally be able to put our hearts and minds in order. Thank you, Jenn J.!

True, cloth sacks are not an original idea; my apartment is full of them, they have found their way into shoe and book purchases, at book fairs and festivals, and stores selling high-end clothes. Yet nevertheless, although they aren't original, Jenn's little bags and sacks are aesthetically irresistible, like brightly colored candy or Christmas tree ornaments, and there is no cynical jab with which one could undercut Jenn's concept, especially because the bags are sewn from cloth made of natural fibers, as we're told by socially sensitive Jenn J. Her sacks and bags are not sewn by sickly little waifs in Bangladesh, but by Jenn herself, this beautiful and sensual woman at her sewing machine, surrounded by the enchanting, colorful textiles and her sylphlike daughters. Plastic bags pollute the environment, while when we buy Jenn's, we'll have them for our lifetime. From time to time we can refresh our collection, and if we tire of the ones we have, we can always rip out the seams and use the cloth for curtains, a skirt or—a bigger bag. Oh, yes, and Jenn J. has been selling her bags online, but recently she opened an eco-friendly store in Manhattan. The store was designed by the happy family's dad, making sure to use eco-friendly materials.

What drew my friend so to the cloth bags story? Envy, she confessed. The images of total success compelled her to wonder where she, herself, had gone wrong. My friend has a degree in physics. She soon realized physics would not be putting bread on the table. She tried opening a store like Jenn J. It flopped. Okay, the story was in Belgrade, not Manhattan, but a store is a store. Recently she earned a PhD, no, not in physics, but in communication theory, something about social networks. She's close to fifty, and not a job in sight. True, her husband works, and this salvages the situation—the refrigerator is never empty and the bills are paid on time.

"There, that's why I'd like to interview Jenn J.," says my friend, "I want to ask her what she did that I failed to do, to learn from where I went wrong . . ."

2.

What sort of times are these? I mean, what is this when as soon as they've moved beyond nursery school people plunge straightaway into a midlife crisis, with sleepless nights spent leafing through possible scenarios and options, such as: what would happen if I'd turned right then instead of left? Or some down instead of up? Under Communism, a person could always blame the system, Communism itself; under capitalism we are all to blame for our own shortcomings. Hence the sleepless nights, or the falling sound asleep as if our sleep will catapult us into a better future or better past. Jenn J. does not have Brezhnev's thick eyebrows, or Stalin's mustache, nor does she look as if she has just stepped out of a massage parlor, the way so many oligarchs, crooks, murderers, thieves, tycoons, scum, and riffraff—in short, people in government—look. Jenn J. is soothing with her air of cute, innocent housewife whose only worry in the world is her family and their quality of life. Enthralled by the images of the happiness of a family for whom every day is Christmas, my Swedish friend is not able to answer the question of how it's possible to afford a house on Manhattan's Upper West Side, a storefront in Soho, and a charming wooden cottage somewhere in northern Europe, all from selling cloth bags online. And does the answer even matter?

I do understand my friend. I, too, spend sleepless nights wondering where I went wrong. I have my university degrees, I have done and still do my job, and maintain exacting professional, artistic, and moral standards. Where did I go wrong? I muse. I follow the Croatian media and often see faces I knew from my past life. There they are, people I used to know, at a reception or a concert, they are cuddling a cute little poodle in their lap—a vibrating dildo with silken white fur. I see a self-satisfied smile on their faces, not a trace of doubt that they might have taken a wrong turn. I see two men I know; they are dumping water on each other for one bucket challenge or another. I recognize people I know everywhere, they are all successful, they exude absolute satisfaction with themselves and their lives. How is this possible, I wonder, where did I stray off the beaten track, where have I spent all these years, in what fog?

I'd forgotten about one of them; there wasn't much to remember him by—we went to school together in a small, muddy town that had little to boast of but a factory where the locals worked. The man was from one of the muddy villages on the outskirts of the muddy factory town. His parents were farmers, barely literate. He'd squeaked by with a degree in economics, came back, and found a job at the factory. Joining the Communist party just as it was on its last legs, he was an exemplar of the transition to capitalism, and, again, not especially memorable. Today, some forty-five years later, I read in a Croatian news source that he's director of the factory, which he has been nibbling at, bite by bite, until he wolfed it all down like a chocolate bar. And he bought a massive villa in London, in Hampstead Heath. I wonder how he knew, that kid from the muddy village, how did he pull that off? Why didn't I think of such a thing? Wasn't I smarter than him, how didn't I get it? Where did I go wrong?

Where did I go wrong, a friend of mine asked, an astrophysicist. He was left jobless, and scrolled through his computer to find something, anything, to make ends meet. There before him on the computer screen loomed Kim Kardashian's large, oiled butt. The butt wasn't moving, it watched my friend like a meteorite, a glacier, a star . . . Kim Kardashian's butt came jumping off every website, the world over, wherever he clicked. My friend realized this butt was the final greeting from a civilization breathing its last, and he relaxed. The Kardashian meteorite came slowly closer, in another second it would crash into Earth and shatter into a million bits. Where have I gone wrong, asked the astrophysicist with the last vestiges of his brain.

Where did I go wrong? It can't be all that hard, especially if kids are more adept than I am at managing life! How could I never have gotten around to writing my autobiography, when fifteen-year-olds were already writing theirs. *My Life So Far* . . . Zoella, a young stylist, makeup artist, vlogger, began her innocuous, chatty vlog with advice for little girls on how to put on makeup, do hair. And surprise, surprise, millions of likes, millions of clicks, and hardly a few months went by when Penguin published her book, *Girl Online*. The book was written by their editors. Famous Zoella, aka Zoe Sugg, said, "Of course I was going to have help from Penguin's editorial team in telling my story."

Where did I go wrong, asked my friend, Dr. Dado. He was nearly 50, a general practitioner with two unfinished residencies behind him, working in urgent care in a little provincial town near Zagreb, driving to work every day, with a two-hour commute in each direction. True, traffic was partly to blame, but along the way he'd stop in to see at least five people: an elderly grandmother, a friend who needed a shot (the friend's physician refused to make house calls), a neighbor who couldn't get to the pharmacy on his own, but who needed the medicine . . . Where did I go wrong, asked his wife. She had a degree in electrical engineering, one of the more challenging university programs, a straight-A student, found a job in a secondary vocational school as a teacher and couldn't land a better job. So now the two of them and their beagle make do, in their minuscule Novi Zagreb apartment; they still haven't paid off their mortgage, and are finding it tricky to get around their place because their books are crowding them out. "We've had to make do with so little," they say. "How can we give up our books!"

3.

Where did I go wrong? In the forty years I've been writing, we've reached the point where hardly anyone buys serious books anymore, and if they do, the buyers are offered a bonus, a sample packet of instant coffee along with the book. On sugar packets—which even children, and almost zero adults, hardly use any more—the attentive café customer will discover the occasional verse of poetry, printed in tiny letters . . .

"Do you know what it says on one series of the bags?" asks my friend.
"What bags?"
"Jenn's little sacks, remember?"
"Oh yes! What?"
"Great minds discuss ideas, average minds discuss events, small minds discuss people."
"Who said that?"
"Eleanor Roosevelt."

"And?"

"That woman is brilliant!"

"Who? Eleanor Roosevelt?"

"No, no. Jenn J."

"Why?"

"Because the world is going to hell! Jenn J. is going to start making eco-friendly body bags soon. They'll come in handy for burials, once people start dying en masse of hunger or World War III . . . People are, after all, eco-friendly manure! Can you imagine the three hundred superrich on Earth having something else in mind?"

December 2014

Unhappiness Is Other People

The mission of folly, to all appearances, is universal in the higher, rain-drenched, non-ideologized meaning of the word: folly is a celestial force acting like gravity or light, like water, and, generally, like one of the elements of the universe.

Miroslav Krleža, *On the Edge of Reason*

1.

Someone recently asked me about moments in my life when I have felt pure happiness. I was devastated by the question. The word *happiness* is not part of my vocabulary, and the question of whether or not I'm happy is one I haven't asked myself for some thirty years. Moments of happiness are few and far between, I stammered, knowing full well that I was buying time. Only a person of a certain age dares allow themselves platitudes such as: *moments of happiness are few and far between.* I realize I must have reached that age. Age is my crutch.

The pious have an easier time of it. No matter what awful things they do, from filching a wallet to murder, God is close at hand to forgive and forget. The faithful jettison their heavy burdens and, light as a feather, move on. And there you have it, a viable reason for happiness! I, myself, am not religious; I am one of that negligible number. I do believe in the unproven claim that this is still the best of all possible worlds.

But the minute I'd uttered that liquid platitude, I did recall a moment of pure happiness. I should say I am not a professional hunter for happiness by any means, I pursue no hobbies that might have a high happiness quotient; I am no alpinist or yodeler. I am a dark-minded, urban human being and my moments of happiness are, indeed, few and far between.

It was when I was a teenager, maybe seventeen, and we were spending the summer on the Black Sea. I was not a bad swimmer, although on the Black Sea everyone dares to feel bold: there are no sharks there, though the undertow sometimes pulls swimmers out into deeper waters. For that very reason there were watchtowers and teams of lifeguards along the Black Sea beaches (something like a live Bulgarian *Baywatch*, but with no Pamela Anderson); well, at least they were there under Communism, at a time when the lives of the communist masses were thought to be worth saving. How things stand now I couldn't say. I was with friends that day on an untended beach—no watchtowers, no lifeguards. And so it was that I found myself quite far out at sea with the sun blazing high above. At first I was overwhelmed by an intense bliss, but soon quieted down, found a kind of tranquility, and floated for a time. And then *through me* (yes, that's how I'd describe it) passed a school of fish that kept coming, seemingly without end. I felt as if liquid silver were sliding through me, I was "theirs," I was a big fish and they were a mass of millions of small fry. I wasn't afraid, I enjoyed it, at that moment I felt as if I were yet another species of fish. I glanced over at the shore, and in the distance I could just make out the figure of a swimmer. After a time I was able to make out the face of my friend, who had set out to help me. Together we returned to shore. The tide tossed us out a mile or two from where we'd started.

The other moment of happiness that I remember is also linked to the sea. I was spending the summer, about twenty years ago, on the island of Lastovo on the Adriatic. There were no tourists, the war had ended only shortly before, and I swam, completely alone, in a deserted little cove. Suddenly, some fifty feet from me, a dolphin leaped out of the water. The sight was absolutely breathtaking: the vast shimmering body, the spraying droplets of water lit by the sun! I felt my heart— whether from terror or joy—tighten into a little ball the size of a strawberry. The dolphin vanished and I made for shore.

Yes, I know, it's difficult to feel respect for a person whose moments of pure happiness are all about marine life. To be honest I'm not sure how to explain it. I have nothing against the fish and mammals of the deep, but I have nothing for them either. Fish and I generally encounter each other in the customary executioner-victim constellation: they on the serving dish, just off the grill, me at my plate, fork in hand. So I'm left with the conclusion that these moments of pure joy are really about being in water, a return to a primeval psyche we can no longer recall but our genes still sense. Who knows how many millions of years ago that was—that primeval state of mind when we were living all together, the species existing then and those which hadn't yet evolved into being, mingling as if at a hot springs where admission was free of charge.

2.

Now, were I to publish these lines in the Croatian press, somebody would swiftly attack me for defining happiness in terms of Communism, because I mentioned "a hot spring where admission was free of charge," I am championing "equality among all beings on Earth," and instead of addressing fish and dolphins as might a fisherman or a sailor, I am championing the "brotherhood and unity" of all living species, including the fish swimming in the waters off Bulgaria! And Bulgaria, isn't that practically Serbia, anyway? It doesn't take long to see why the word "happiness" vanished from my vocabulary. All because of stupidity!

For years I have been dwelling in an empire of stupidity. Stupidity has become, over time, far too burdensome for me. I am finding it difficult to breathe under its weight and cannot shake free of it. I tried for a while with laughter, and, to be sure, that helped. But now stupidity has barged in, made itself at home, and soaked up all the oxygen. A quarter century ago, stupidity grabbed the microphone, gleeful with self-confidence, and hogged center stage. There is no hope that it will be relinquishing its position any time soon. Into the microphone it squawks and squawks, and demands of me that I listen and voice my admiration for it. Stupidity has strode in through the front door over this last quarter century—straight into nursery schools, elementary and secondary schools, and universities. Meanwhile, stupidity has raised new generations of offspring who are swiftly taking charge. Stupidity has elbowed its way into the press, the media, even into my humdrum realm of literature. Stupidity pens its own autobiographies, and promotes and awards the literary critics who offer it their support. Stupidity took from me and many others our workplaces and threw us out into the streets. People who were once chauffeurs, electricians, petty crooks, murderers, plumbers, truck drivers, journalists, and professors (some of consequence, others of none), psychiatrists, military generals, historians, grifters, con artists, and card sharks—they knew how to rob us blind and ride our backs. Stupidity reigns and won't give us room to breathe. When somebody complains, stupidity kicks up a huge fuss and looses its shrieks from thousands and thousands of righteous throats. The din is unbearable.

Stupidity is forever whining and moaning, stupidity needles like a toothache, stupidity is rapacious, it always feels it deserves better. Stupidity struts its patriotism and thinks that for its volunteer effort of loving its homeland it should receive full financial compensation. The Croatian volunteers, war veterans, receive state pensions. Some of these pensions are as much as ten times the average Croatian income. Militarized stupidity has, at times, taken to the streets of Zagreb to demand even more. It turns out that these volunteers—the invalids, both genuine and fraudulent, the warriors, both genuine and fraudulent, the male masqueraders sporting black T-shirts with big white crosses on the chest

(Croatian crusaders!), or checkerboard scarves in Croatia's national colors—have the right idea. For who could possibly love this country—or any country like it, for that matter—free of charge!

Stupidity has a penchant for funerals. Much like the Italian mafia of American movies, the people of the Balkans are big on the art of funerals and burials. Recently, it seems as if Croats can hardly wait for someone to die, and then they fling themselves into keening and wailing. The dramatic images of people fainting, reciting speeches, shedding copious public tears, provide the media with grist for their mill. Top-notch journalists crank out reams of paper soaked with authentic tears. There are people who get two send-offs: a popular singer who recently died was given one funeral where he lived, and another where he was born. The high artistic and dramatic bar for funerals was set by Tito's "gravediggers." None has outshone Franjo Tuđman in this respect. His burial was the most splendid. Croats adore funerals. At funerals they go all-out to mourn and grieve for themselves, the "sorry wretches" left behind.

And as I click my way with my TV remote from channel to channel I see scenes of funerals, scenes of the fetching lads, those war veterans, some of them standing, others in wheelchairs, bent on broadcasting to the world their message: that their homeland is not worth defending for free. I see scenes of the Croatian president as she is borne aloft by Croatian voters (in their thoughts, of course), much the way the Catholic faithful carry icons of the Mother of God on pilgrimages (it should be said that all the Balkan peoples are famous for adoring their political leaders). And suddenly this whole "glorious" struggle of ex-Yugoslav peoples and ethnicities for independence, freedom, statehood, national identity, and so forth spreads out before my eyes like a *reality TV show*: a dynamic landscape of depravity, murder, the theft and expropriation of big and little houses, native soil and whole hillsides, gold ducats and ready cash, checking and savings accounts, pots of gold and barrels of wine, factories and franchises, gas stations and hotels, villas and estates, seats in parliament and ambassadorial posts.

And what about the rest of us who have wasted a good portion of our lives describing the *reality show*, high entertainment that it is, of others, as our own deeply humiliating reality? What about all of us? For we, in one way or another, have all been and remain hostages of stupidity, whether we have shined its shoes, or believed we were conduits for enlightenment, or were living in silence in an underground reality off the political grid. In better times, the police simply switch the *reality show* off. When times are bad, the high courts of Croatia and Serbia exonerate the war criminals, murderers, and swindlers.

Several times now I have cited the memorable words a little girl uttered during the shelling of Sarajevo. She was in the city hospital's psychiatric ward. "What are you the most afraid of," asked the doctors. "People," she said. The little girl must be a young woman now, nearly thirty. I hope she has learned to live with her fears. Unhappiness is other people—this is the first assumption one must be guided by when living among them. Many years have passed since then, enough for devastated lives, for healing wounds, for forgetting fears.

Twenty-three years have passed since Operation Storm. In the intervening years, many of the homes of Serbs who fled in 1995 were burned to the ground, and other people moved into the empty houses that remained standing. Except for the most persistent, few of the Serbs who fled in 1995 have been able to regain the right to their property and move back to Croatia. Middle-aged returnees, Dušan and Mara Novaković, moved back recently and were stripped of their property for a second time. Somebody set fire to their village home. Their first neighbor gets scared at night: "I lock the door and am terrified whenever I hear a dog barking. We aren't scared any more of wild animals, it's people we're afraid of," she said.[5]

The creators of the Netflix series *Zoo*—in which the animals, tired of the terror visited upon them by people, join forces in a global animal resistance movement—understood this. The scenes in which lions, tigers, elephants, rhinoceroses, and even the smaller members of the animal kingdom bare their teeth, filling me with a particular satisfaction. I side, in any case, with the animals. As I said at the beginning, I swim with the fish.

2015–2018

5 Paulina Arbutina, "Gori vatra" [A Fire Is Burning]. *Novosti*, 31 May 2018.

Invisible Europe

Fish and women, books and music, religious faith and the law, world view and poetry, all of these are bartered in Europe for cash, and today currency, instead of the person, is the sole parameter, the only scales, the sole endorsement of human qualities . . .

Miroslav Krleža, *Europe Today*, 1935

1.

I'm not one to pay much attention to dreams. But this dream I remembered, though only its blueprint. The details and nuances change with the telling. I have preserved the blueprint and have been carrying it with me for a quarter century now like mental baggage I can't seem to shed. The doorbell rings at my Zagreb apartment. I open the door and people I've never seen before come pouring in. "Who are you? How dare you barge in without my say-so?" I shout. "This is my apartment!" A woman, meanwhile, is changing her baby's diaper on my bed, a man goes into my bathroom ("Hey, that's my bathroom!"), somebody opens the fridge and begins rummaging for food ("How dare you! That's my refrigerator!"), I fume and threaten ("I'll call the police!"), but they don't hear me. I'm invisible to them. My apartment fills with people and nothing seems to stop them. "How can so many of them fit in here! As if they're not people but a deck of cards!" I think in my dream.

A few months after I dreamt this, war broke out in Yugoslavia, my country. Tens of thousands of refugees dispersed across the globe, some even finding their way to Afghanistan. With a freshly issued, only just valid passport from the newly minted state of Croatia, I left my country. Or I should say my country left me. I know now that the hundreds and hundreds of thousands of refugees who are knocking at the doors of Europe did not leave their countries. Their countries left them.

No matter what we call them—guided by the etiquette of political correctness—whether emigrants or émigrés, migrants, refugees, exiles, or asylum-seekers, we all know about whom we're talking. This is our shared cultural *meme*. European, Christian civilization began with people seeking refuge. All of us have internalized the image of God banishing Adam and Eve from paradise, irately wagging his index finger. The image is a part of our lasting cultural legacy. I set out into the world when the then president of Croatia—with that same godly ease and menacing finger—announced he was the "Croatian George Washington" and declared Croatia to be "heaven on earth." Today, when I watch jihadist videos, I note that they are ever-ready to wag that finger.

Wielding it like a sword, they threaten gruesome punishments on those who refuse to obey.

We all have refugees as part of our mental vocabulary: the notions of *expulsion, exodus, exile,* are built into the very foundations of our civilization and personal lives. Yet we tend to close our eyes to the numbers (at the end of 2014, some 60 million people had been displaced, the most since World War II), to the images of the dead bodies washing up on the shores of Italy, Spain, and Greece, to scenes from refugee ghettos, to the island of Lampedusa—one of the symbolic topoi of the "migration crisis."

Marjola Rukaj, Albanian photographer, takes portraits of refugees, but also the small things the refugees bring with them, with all their charged symbolic potential. She snaps shots of cell phones, trinkets, a ribbon, a bracelet, a necklace . . . When examining one of Rukaj's photographs, the blood froze in my veins. The picture was of an inexpensive necklace and, dangling from it, a razor blade charm. I experienced the razor blade as a miniature passport allowing the crossing of the last border, between the world of the living and the world of the dead, an exit, as if into death, a poisonous snake we carry with us like a pet, to be set free from the cage only once and never more.

While we choose to look the other way, migrants are trundling along, with superhuman strength and tenacity. According to a report by the Norwegian government, in November of 2015, more than four thousand migrants crossed the narrow Norwegian–Russian border, thereby opening a new and unexpected "artic route."

Russian law forbids traversing the last dozen miles on foot, so they covered those last miles riding children's bicycles over the frozen expanses. Perhaps some of them riding bicycles warmed themselves with visions of the lights of Paris, unaware that at that very moment, on November 13, 2015, terrorists had turned Paris into a site of bloodshed, violence, and fear. Reality becomes fantasy at this point. Life is not a dream, life is cinema, the *hunger games*.

No doubt many of my former countrymen—themselves refugees twenty years ago and now law-abiding taxpayers in Western European countries—are dead set against the idea of this new wave of refugees becoming their fellow citizens. The countries that stepped out from behind the Iron Curtain, such as Hungary, Bulgaria, and Romania, have since hastened to raise new—barbed-wire—curtains, without a thought to the fact that a Hungarian, Romanian, or Bulgarian child, not just a Syrian child, could become entangled in the wire. Countries like Serbia, Croatia, and Slovenia over the last several years have been treating refugees like tennis balls for their games of petty, local, embittered political matches.

A large portion of today's world is tightrope walking. It is difficult to say on which side these tightrope walkers will fall or whether they will fall at all. The landscape is not attractive, down below are fields sprouting rolls of barbed wire and swastikas, and the view of the other shore is murky at best. Nobody can guarantee there isn't a crazed suicide-bomber crouching there on the opposite, well-lit shore. Nobody can tell yet whether tightrope walking is the new lifestyle, the new code, the new morals, the new politics. Terrorism is amoral, as Jean Baudrillard declared after September 11th. Have we, the citizens of the world, been so overcome by fear that we, too, have become amoral?

Europa was, herself, a migrant; according to one mythical version she was the daughter of a Phoenician king, born in the city of Tyre in what is today Lebanon, and astride a bull—her lover, Zeus—she reached the shores of Europe. Reaching the opposite shore astride a bull is every bit as spectacular as riding across the last dozen miles of ice on a child's bike.

Refugees and migrants serve as a mirror, a test, a challenge, a summons to confront *our* values. The events, some of them visible, others less so, which have followed since the "migrant crisis" was identified, are being added to the collage. The people fleeing their countries are the beginning and end, the cause and effect, they are the deck of cards from which the near future of the world will be read. And whoever knows how to read these cards will know what lies ahead.

2.

I don't know when it was that I first met Meliha, a Bulgarian woman who cleans apartments in Amsterdam. All I remember is that she introduced herself as Meli . . .

"Meli isn't a Bulgarian name, is it?" I asked.

"Well not everyone who comes from Bulgaria is . . . Bulgarian," she said cautiously.

Meli's background was Bulgarian-Turkish. She was from a far-flung village somewhere in the northeastern end of the country.

Her parents apparently did little but have children, producing a brood of seventeen. Three of us died, said Meliha, and fourteen of us are left. Carried away with their procreational vigor, the parents seem to have failed to note that in Communist Bulgaria they'd had decent health care, readily available contraception, and the right to abortion. Having spent his reproductive role, her father died like a salmon after spawning. Her mother, the queen bee, lives the life of a fertility goddess: her children look after her and after one another, the older ones raising the younger.

Meliha and her four sisters were renting an apartment together in Amsterdam. They were all working as house cleaners and all also had jobs at Albert Heijn, the largest and best-known Dutch supermarket chain. Albert Heijn is such a powerful company that they put a supermarket up in the middle of Museum Square in Amsterdam, rubbing elbows with the three cultural giants: the Van Gogh Museum, the Rijksmuseum, and the Stedelijk. Albert Heijn is the fourth "giant," it keeps an eye on museum visitors, passersby, and denizens of the Museum neighborhood. Many, having purchased a bottle of water and a sandwich at the supermarket, recline on its architecturally appealing, slanted grassy roof.

Meli and her sisters cleaned the supermarket twice a week, and they reported this part of their earnings to the Dutch tax collectors. Their regular payment of taxes would be key on the day when they went to the Dutch authorities to request Dutch citizenship. Meli arrived in the Netherlands at the age of nineteen; now she is twenty-eight. She was born in the year the Berlin Wall fell. This detail meant something to me but little to her. She works every day from morning till night, and stops by my place when she can, on Sundays.

Meli barely has a fourth-grade education. She has never traveled around Bulgaria, she's never been to Sofia, the closest being the Sofia Airport from where she flies to Amsterdam. She cycles through the streets of Amsterdam like a true Dutch woman. And when she stops by my place to visit I often sit her down at my computer. We work on the basics, the names of the capital cities and countries of Europe . . .

"How can you not know! You need to know where you are in the world," I insist. She laughs. Her smile exposes a sharp tooth growing over another tooth.

"And you should go to the dentist, for God's sake, to have that tooth taken care of!"

She laughs again. She has no intention whatsoever of going to the dentist.

Meliha and I speak in Bulgarian. Her Bulgarian is not fluent. Mine isn't much better. Mine was left behind somewhere in my childhood, I learned what I knew while I visited my grandparents, my mother's parents, who lived in Varna. With their death, our family vacations on the Black Sea also came to an end. Meliha has never been to the Black Sea. Just like her sisters, she bought a house in her village and a small apartment in a nearby town. She rents out the apartment. Meliha is a successful young woman, especially if one considers what her chances for success were to begin with. She renovated her house according to urban standards. Thanks to her ties to Bulgarian trucking, she managed to arrange to have all the furniture she'd bought in Amsterdam delivered to her village. Everything in her house is now brand spanking new.

"I'll come see this miracle for myself," I say.

"Come," she says, and laughs.

"Once you've put in a jacuzzi."

She laughs; she has plans for a jacuzzi.

3.

Frank is a handyman. He tore down walls in my apartment, removed all the rubble, and prepped the apartment for the electricians, plumbers, and other tradespeople. He did this all in three days, for a surprisingly modest sum. And over those three days I learned that Frank was the son of a Dutch Protestant minister, he'd been married, had no children, was well-educated and had a job, and then one day he abruptly decided to abandon it all. He closed his bank accounts, his tax numbers, his phone numbers, he unregistered his addresses, and completely removed himself from the system. The jobs he did as a handyman he found through people he knew. Frank's girlfriend's phone number was Frank's only contact point. I paid him with a pang of guilt, I felt he was charging too little. We said our goodbyes. For some reason I thought I'd never see him again.

With no forewarning, Frank showed up at my door some fifteen years later. He joined me for coffee and we talked. In the meanwhile he'd bought a house in a far-flung mountain village in southern Bulgaria, near the Turkish border. And his girlfriend is there with him. He helps the villagers build and repair their homes and, in return, the villagers teach him how to work the land, cultivate vegetables, set up beehives . . .

"So what are you doing in Amsterdam?" I asked.

His Dutch passport had expired, and without a passport he couldn't travel; he was worried he might have difficulty renewing it, because the Dutch authorities could no longer find a single item in his file but his birth certificate to prove that he was a Dutch citizen. Frank had done far too thorough a job, apparently, at removing himself from the system.

A Bulgarian woman in the Netherlands, a Dutch man in Bulgaria—these are only two of the millions of similar stories of today's Europe. If there is anything truly relevant in the current inflation of intellectual narratives about European identity, a European future, the European crisis, Europe after the wall, new European walls—then it should be the narrative of the magnificent, extraordinary circulation of human material. *Human cargo.* Wars, murders, genocides, political systems, states and borders, ideological and religious systems, nationalisms—all this pales in comparison to the fates of ordinary people. Sure, if Frank had moved to Bulgaria during the Communist years, maybe he wouldn't have needed a Dutch passport anymore, maybe he'd never have been able to leave Bulgaria again. Sure, if Yugoslavia hadn't come apart at the seams, if a mob of brutal thugs, elected by the democratic majority, hadn't grabbed hold of power, I wouldn't have ended up in Amsterdam and I would never have made the acquaintance of Frank and Meli. Nor would Meli have ended up in Amsterdam if Bulgaria had not become a member of the European Union, followed by the transition and state-run thievery that brought

Bulgarian citizens to the verge of starvation. Meli is not in Amsterdam for the tourism, Meli is here to feed herself and her large family, which was brought into the world by her carefree, childish parents. Whatever the case, the entire world relies for its existence on carefree, childish parents.

4.

Goran is a general practitioner. He moved to Amsterdam from Belgrade. He started studying medicine there, met a Dutch woman, they married, the war broke out in Yugoslavia, the country fell apart, but thanks to his marriage he was able to obtain a new passport, complete his studies in the Netherlands, find a job here, settled down, have kids . . . In the blink of an eye his children were grown, had embarked on their own university studies, left home . . .

"I'm going to die," he moaned over the phone.

"Why?"

"I'm working too hard."

As usual, he didn't listen to me.

"The only thing that can save me is the dog . . ."

"Dog?"

"The one I adopted."

"You adopted a dog?"

"A mutt."

"A puppy?"

"No, it's twelve."

"Well what's the point of a geriatric canine?"

"It'll die soon."

"Then why adopt it?"

"So I could have something to care for."

"You have your patients to care for."

"That's different . . ."

And he told me he'd joined a network of good people who were adopting dogs from Eastern Europe. They'd heard pets were being abandoned because the people there couldn't afford to feed them. In Bucharest, I saw for myself that dogs were roaming free in the city center, lazily sunning in packs, loping around at night on the lookout for food. Sometimes they even attacked people.

"So why not adopt a child?"

Why should he adopt a child when sooner or later he'd have grandchildren of his own? Dogs were better. When they weren't barking they were quiet, they made no demands, they weren't violent, didn't remonstrate, didn't lie, offered instant moral gratification, didn't expect unconditional love the way children did . . .

I understand him, I know all about displacement, this particular brand of refugee, émigré, exile, migrant neurosis. He'd spent half his life dreaming he'd go back, though he wanted to go back to Croatia, not Serbia. He longed to move to the Adriatic Coast, he, a man from Belgrade, who'd settled in Amsterdam. What would he do in Croatia? He'd practice medicine on an island. He'd spent years searching for houses and islands. And then finally he found heaven on earth, the island of Mljet. He submitted his application to a job posted there for a general practitioner. Nobody could hold a candle to him: he was conversant in Dutch, Italian, German, English, and almost all the languages of the peoples of ex-Yugoslavia (beneficial both for tourists needing medical care and the locals), and he had certificates in scuba diving (if something were to happen to someone underwater), speleology (for anyone trapped in a cave), and a license to operate a motorboat (in case somebody had to be transferred to a mainland hospital in Split or Dubrovnik). He did not get the job. "I did my damnedest to use Zagreb slang," he said without a trace of irony.

He is discombobulated, that's the long and the short of it. Wherever you go you need to adapt, to sit in a bread mold like dough. He failed at this. He's torn, he keeps up with current events and remembers how things used to be, he's not young but he's not old, he is practical yet romantic, many things rub him wrong, hurt him, he often hops into his car and drives to Italy, from Italy he motors on through ex-Yugoslavia, through Slovenia, Croatia, zips down the coast, dips into Bosnia, then goes off to Serbia (to visit his aging parents), he treats his neurosis by racking up the mileage on his car. I understand him. *Horror vacui.* He is tormented by a metaphysical itch. The doctor is seeking meaning in his life, he's looking for "furniture" to keep at bay the anxiety stirred by the empty space around him. And inside him. For as a doctor he knows best that the meaning of life lies in the fact that it—life—will, one day, end. Putting a stop to any and all deal making. Period.

5.

Meliha has an iPhone, the most recent, expensive model. She shows me pictures of a wedding. Of her ten sisters she will soon be the only one who isn't married. The weddings are grand, expensive, with a long guest list and shimmering dresses. One of Meliha's sisters married a Turkish man in Istanbul. The wedding was colossal. They found a groom for Meliha as well, but he wasn't worth mentioning, a creep . . . And this other one, whose picture she shows me on the screen, handsome, muscular, with a modern haircut ending in a cowlick on his forehead . . .

"Now that one likes to be in charge," I say, touching his picture on the screen tentatively, with two fingers as if it were a dead mouse.

"True," she says. Meliha may be short on experience, but her discerning eye ticks like a Swiss watch.

Bulgarians, it should be said, have, at times, humiliated their Turks, the two million of them who were living in Bulgaria, compelling them to work the nastiest and most poorly paid jobs, and change their name and faith. Now Bulgarian women do the same work in Istanbul as Meli does in Amsterdam, as Croatian, Serbian, Romanian, and Albanian women do in Italy, as Slovakian women do in Austria, as Lithuanian women do in Switzerland, as . . .

And while the European political bureaucracy spreads its wings in Brussels, and while prominent political thinkers fling philosophical mortar now and then at the ideological construct of Europe, and while petty European Fascists settle into European commissions like nesting hens, clucking loudly and every so often producing a "serpent's egg," and while in many countries transitioning between Communism and capitalism there is not so much as the letter D left of democracy, everyday European life continues to push in various directions, and on invisible cyber-papyrus, millions of European human fates are being recorded.

What happened with Meli was a miracle. She, who'd been so reticent simply because she had a vocabulary of barely five hundred words, she whom I'd coached on European geography, she had learned to speak Dutch. I'd never have known she'd mastered it on the sly if Dutch friends of mine hadn't stopped by one Sunday while Meli was visiting. She conversed with them in Dutch with real eloquence. That Sunday, in the presence of my friends, it was hard to stop her. Meli's self-decolonization happened in language, through language, thanks to language. This is why I'm beginning to think she will never go back. Where can she go back to? A native language where the best she can do is stutter?

6.

Europe is rife with paradoxes. Paradoxes are what keep it alive. This, of course, is not something that those who build the barbed-wire walls and fences know about, they're convinced they are in charge. During Operation Storm, for which Croats feel particular pride, they expelled thousands of Serbs. Ten years hence the population of Croats began to shrink. Right now, the shrinking is accelerating from one month to the next. Croats are leaving the country, *heaven on earth*, in search of better jobs, and this is not the first time this has happened in their modest history. Whoever can is fleeing, those with little or no schooling, those with plenty of schooling, the young, the old . . . They are going wherever they are welcome: Ireland, Denmark, the Faroe Islands. Such as one young Slavonian man, Ivan, whom I sat next to on a flight to Zagreb last Christmas. He couldn't have been much over eighteen, a manual laborer, he mixed mortar, carried bricks . . .

"How's that going for you in the Faroes?"

"Great, there are plenty of people there from around here . . . It's just a bit on the cold side," he said and laughed.

When he talks, he swallows parts of words and compensates by drawling the rest, as do people from Slavonia. He speaks, though he is clearly unused to conversation, words confuse him, yet I feel he enjoys being the center of somebody's attention, no matter how fleeting or random. He's going to his village, going home for the Christmas holidays, and then he'll return to the Faroes . . .

"So what will you do while you're in Slavonia?"

"Dunno, I'll have me a look-see . . ."

"What will you have a look at when you just told me your parents died and you have no family left?"

"Well, I don't . . ."

"Why go?"

"To see how the house is doing . . ."

"But you said your house is crumbling and there's no electricity . . ."

"Well, I don't . . ."

"So what will you do there?"

"Dunno, have me a look-see . . ." the young man dug in his heels and a hard expression flitted across his face like a shadow.

At that moment, in the plane as it was landing at Zagreb Airport, I felt as if the young man, too, was a shadow, like Meliha, and like Frank became after he took himself off the grid. They, like millions of others, lead parallel lives. These are people with no voice yet they are motivating, advancing, and sustaining European life. They are invisible Europe.

7.

George Steiner, one of the last towering figures of European intellectual life with a strong humanist bent, in his oft-cited *The Idea of Europe* enumerates five postulates that define Europe. The first is the *café*, as a place for creating and exchanging intellectual values. Indeed, Europe is crisscrossed by cafés that are key to the cultural and intellectual history of Europe. Take the Odeon, for instance, in Zurich. A glance at its clientele, which included Franz Werfel, Stefan Zweig, Frank Wedekind, Karl Kraus, William Somerset Maugham, Erich Maria Remarque, Klaus Mann, James Joyce, Hans Arp, Tristan Tzara, Hugo Ball, Franz Lehár, Arturo Toscanini, Albert Einstein, Vladimir I. Lenin, and Leon Trotsky, bears out George Steiner's assertion. The second criterion is *geography* or *walkability*, the *human scale*. One can master the distances in European cities and countries on foot. The third parameter, which sets Europe apart from other geographic constellations, is the constant *commemoration of the cultural past* or reminders of it. Streets, squares, and buildings in European cities bear the names of major European writers, philosophers, painters, scientists, and statesmen, reminding us of how inextricably interwoven the European past and present are. The fourth axiom on which the idea of Europe relies is the interweaving of two primordial traditions of civilization, *the dual origins of Europe*, where, metaphorically put, one parent comes from ancient Athens, the other from Jerusalem. The fifth criterion underpinning the idea of Europe and the European is a continual awareness of a *possible end to European civilization*, the presentiment of this end, the awareness of the potential apocalypse. The presentiment of the end is not merely a subject for the ruminations of philosophers such as Spengler and Hegel; it has its roots in the European experience of the two world wars, the Holocaust, and mass destruction. Hundreds of millions of people were killed in these wars, six million European Jews were murdered in the Holocaust. Many parts of Europe were razed to the ground. The firm commitment never to let this happen again was flouted by the relatively recent "Yugoslav" wars (1991–2001), in which, as if the warring parties were following a textbook, many of the same things were repeated: the ethnic cleansing, the destruction, the expulsion, the genocide (Srebrenica), the camps, the forced resettlement, and the refugees.

Steiner—who senses the pending European collapse, the onslaught of the barbarians and the ebb of European ideas—seeks a way out through cultural utopia, through dreaming a new dream of enlightenment, through focusing on things of little utility, and on truths. "The dignity of *Homo sapiens* is exactly that: the realization of wisdom, the pursuit of disinterested knowledge, the creation of beauty. Making money and flooding our lives with increasingly trivialized material goods is a profoundly vulgar, emptying passion." Steiner condemns the "despotism of the mass-market and the rewards of commercialized stardom" because of which the best minds of Europe are embracing "the Edenic offers of the United States."[6]

At the rare moments where Steiner lapses into a typical European lament, the reader might stop and recall just how much Europeans have gained from the idea of America. And how much America

---

6 George Steiner, *The Idea of Europe*. 2015. London: Overlook Duckworth: 63-64.

itself has gained from the many émigrés who moved there from Europe. Perhaps there is relevance in a story told by a guide on a tour boat on which I cruised around Manhattan a few years ago, about how the eastern shoreline of Manhattan was fortified with rubble transported from Europe during World War II; the empty ships returning to the United States after delivering aid to England would load rubble from the Blitz—the ballast necessary to stabilize the ship. Who knows, maybe the eastern shoreline of Manhattan was built on rubble from Coventry Cathedral! Even if this story isn't true, the metaphor still holds. People didn't flock to America to save their lives, insure a better future, or take advantage of "Edenic offers," but for a set of ideas that America exemplified: the "dream," the simple things of freedom, choice, tolerance . . . America is a land of settlers, it exists thanks to the people who settled there, who are settling there now, and who will settle there. Millions of lives are built into American culture, into the literature, architecture, movies, art, science, medicine, technology. Many of these people came from Europe. There is nothing sadder than a country whose borders are bristling with barbed wire, yet none of the refugees have any intention of staying. Through Greece, Turkey, Serbia, Hungary, Croatia, and other countries, the refugees seek only passage. Bad countries are merely corridors, and the refugees know this better than anyone.

During the time of Yugoslavia, there were many factories, institutes, streets, and schools named after Nikola Tesla. Socialist propaganda and the slogan *Knowledge Is Power* rang out on all sides. Nikola Tesla was a living example that the enlightenment sentiment espoused by Communism was possible. During the recent war the monument to Tesla in Gospić was destroyed, along with his family home and museum. Until recently, Tesla's child-hood home in Smiljan was surrounded by minefields, but now it has been rebuilt and made into a museum. For the tourists, of course. The main square in Gospić used to be called Nikola Tesla Square. Today it is Stjepan Radić Square. Countless squares and streets in Croatia bear the name of Franjo Tuđman, a third-rate politician, and the first president of the Republic of Croatia. The new Zagreb airport is also named after Tuđman. Although he was born in Croatia, Nikola Tesla was ethnically a Serb, which is the main obstacle to his inclusion in the Croatian pantheon. In Serbia, many streets, squares, and schools, as well as the Belgrade airport, bear the name of Nikola Tesla. As far as the Serbs are concerned, Tesla was a Serb.

In the United States, there is a statue to Nikola Tesla at Niagara Falls. The statue, by Yugoslav sculptor Frano Kršinić, was a gift to the United States from Yugoslavia. In New York City, a corner of Bryant Park was recently named Nikola Tesla Corner. A statue has been installed on Long Island at a key site for Tesla's scientific work. There are busts of Tesla at many American universities, including Harvard, Princeton, Columbia, Michigan, and MIT.

This fragment about Tesla confirms the respect for education, science, invention, enlightenment, progress—everything Tesla personified—and which the culture of the United States values far more than they are valued by the cultures from which Nikola Tesla came. Inclusivity—a great idea that still attracts people to America. Walls and barbed wire will not prevent them from making the trek, drawn by the pull of the idea of a better, more humane, creative, and dignified life. Even if they arrive at their destination disappointed, stripped of rights, humiliated, they will do their best to make real the ideal they set out to attain. Maybe they will be invisible, maybe they will not have the right to vote, but they will be the people who sustain life and lift human standards, the standards of the humane. The zero-tolerance policy will sooner or later backfire on those who are advocating for it. It embitters the life of many who have lived here for generations. The true terror begins when we begin to feel there is nowhere left to emigrate to, that all destinations are equally bad. The only hope left for us is that we haven't yet been faced with the last wall. We haven't, have we?

2015–2018

Artists and Murderers

A lively battle I did wage,
For every letter on the page.
When mastering the letter A,
I wrestled with it one whole day.

Primer, 1957

1.

I admit that over the last twenty-five years I have been finding it increasingly difficult in ex-Yugoslavia and other countries
partway through the transition from Communism to capitalism
to find a "home" for my texts, whether whole books or shorter
pieces. I won't go into whether I'd agree to publish a piece of
mine in the mainstream newspapers in Croatia or Serbia. Right
now I am shaken by the fact that no one since the fall of Yugoslavia has even asked. In my "native" Croatia, the newspapers and
magazines have been circumventing me at every turn. Croats are

particularly prickly about their Croatianhood; trample on their Croatianhood and you're treading on a land mine. Led by this logic, one could assume that Serbs might be more welcoming, but, surprisingly, no. Each side keeps a close watch over their Croatianhood or Serbdom. If you don't give a hoot about Serbdom and Croatianhood, and if you're, moreover, a woman, your unpopularity in both these communities is not hard to understand. Oh, right, and I left. Them. These communities. And that is not readily forgiven.

Does this mean that publishing in the countries in transition, the postcommunist countries, is on its last legs? Why no, it appears to be flourishing. Is culture being sold short? No, actually, people are tripping over themselves to support culture. There are at least three international literary festivals and dozens of local ones every year in little Croatia alone. Every one of the tycoons owns their own newspaper, and oligarchs own whole chains of bookstores (Russians are peerless in this), while the wives, lovers, daughters, and sisters of these same tycoons own publishing houses, galleries, museums, or something similar, in any case something "artistic."

So what's wrong with this picture?!

An email arrived the other day from a woman I know in Belgrade. My acquaintance is a writer and, wouldn't you know it, she had observed similar issues:

"To tell you the truth, finding a publisher, at least in my case, is much more difficult than writing the book. And this at a time when there is hardly a soul who HASN'T written a book and published it in Serbia!" she wrote and went on to describe a television show filmed at the Belgrade Book Fair . . . "Sitting there were these caricatures, all crowing at once, holding books on their laps, *their* books, and behind them cooks were cooking, although the show was not a cooking show. The announcer, herself the author of several books, asked them one by one, the singer, the dancer, the drummer, the starlet . . . what they'd written about. A petite woman, her hair bouffant and her manner huffy, sat at the end of the row, tapping her toes. The announcer came over and asked, 'Are you the only one here who doesn't have a book?' The petite lady spat out: 'Not for long!'"

2.

In his book *Nothing Is True and Everything Is Possible*, Peter Pomerantsev writes about the new Russia, the world of criminals, murderers, oligarchs, politicians, millionaires—called the *Forbeses* in new Russian slang—and the gold-diggers, known as *tyolkas*.

"Can anyone be a killer?" Pomerantsev asks Vitali Dyomochka, a murderer and memorable exemplar of contemporary Russian life.

"No. When I was in prison there were men who regretted what they'd done. They wept, went to church. Not everyone has the inner strength to do this. But I do."

"And would you ever return to crime?"

"Nowadays my life is all about art," answered Dyomochka, thinking aloud.

"I often think now I should have gone into politics. . . . I just thought it boring. I didn't realize they used the same methods as us. It's too late now, though. I've dedicated myself to art. If I can't film, I'll write. And you know what the future is, Peter? Comedy."

The portrait of Russian murderer Vitali Dyomochka hit me in a flash of enlightenment and a total eclipse. Of course there's no room left for me! All the space has been taken up by the Vitali Dyomochkas: the killers who have morphed into "artists"! But if I allow for the possibility that murderers can morph into artists, should I also allow for artists morphing into symbolic and real murderers? Do they?

3.

If we run a search, the internet spits out only the scantest information about writers who were also murderers.

William Burroughs, while high on drugs, shot his wife, also high on drugs.

The name Anne Perry is a pseudonym used by Juliet Hulme. Juliet was an Australian fifteen-year-old who helped her friend Pauline Parker kill Pauline's mother, who was supposedly standing in the way of their happiness. The movie *Heavenly Creatures* is based on the story. Five years later, when the girls were released from prison, Juliet moved to England. She later took the name Anne Perry and became a notable writer of historical detective fiction. François Villon was a fifteenth-century writer who is said to have been a thief, a brawler, and who supposedly killed a priest. Villon was banished but then pardoned, after which all trace of him was lost. A philosopher, Louis Althusser, strangled his wife. *The Future Lasts a Long Time* is the book he wrote about it. María Carolina Geel, a Chilean writer, fired several shots into her lover, who was fourteen years her junior. Hans Fallada was a German writer who conspired with his lover, Hanns Dietrich von Necker, to use a romantic duel as camouflage for their suicides.

Von Necker missed; Fallada killed him and then shot himself in the chest, but survived. He was arrested, but was acquitted of murder by reason of insanity and ended up in a psychiatric ward.

Yet almost all the murders committed by this handful of writers are the result of mistakes, clumsiness, or were crimes of passion. Dutch poet Gerrit Achterberg, for example, fell in love with his landlady and harassed her daughter. When the landlady tried to stop him, Achterberg shot and killed her, and wounded her daughter.

Austrian Johann "Jack" Unterweger (and Jack Henry Abbott) belongs to the obverse category of murderers who become artists. Unterweger was a serial killer who murdered a dozen prostitutes. After he spent fifteen years behind bars—where he wrote poems, stories, and a memoir that served as the basis for a movie—Unterweger was released at the urging of prominent Austrian politicians and intellectuals who were inspired by the case of Jean Genet. As soon as he was released, Unterweger again killed several prostitutes, this time along an international trajectory reaching from the Czech Republic and Austria to Los Angeles. For a time he was a fugitive, but ultimately was sentenced to life in prison. He did not live to serve his sentence because he hanged himself as soon as he was jailed. Unterweger inspired filmmakers, actors, composers, and writers, who have based several of their works on his story.

All in all, there is an evident disproportion among murderers and artists: there are many more fledgling writers among murderers than there are murderers among writers. Art has become a frequent reference point in the biographies of criminals, whether this being their creative impulses, as in the earlier quote about Dyomochka, or their passion for collecting art. Criminal acts may be the subject of many works of art, but seldom do the authors of these works actually commit crimes in their everyday lives. Meanwhile, murderers and criminals use art like a shower to wash away their moral contamination. This is why art is so popular. Everybody enjoys a little morality rinse now and then.

4.

All the Balkan scum that has been strutting its feathers before us over the last twenty years—the criminals and murderers, thieves and embezzlers, liars and mafia bosses, generals and soldiers, priests and clergy, politicians and politicos, but also the attorneys, both men and women, who have been successfully defending them—have suddenly, surprise, surprise, been seeking solace in art!

Croatia is a small country with feverish activity in the arts. At the moment, three books and a DVD are holding pride of place at newspaper stands and the occasional bookstore display. The modest selection includes *Famous Croatian Men* (the smaller the country the more famous its men!); Zvonko Bušić Tajko's memoir *The Sharp Eye of Memory*; a book about pop singer Severina with her bare bottom flaunted on the cover; a documentary film about the Ustashas, titled simply *The Ustashas*, by Croatian director Jakov Sedlar, known for his documentary *Franjo Tuđman—the Croatian George Washington.*

So who was this Zvonko Bušić Tajko? He is the one who, with his American girlfriend, Julienne, hijacked a plane en route from Europe to the States to draw the attention of the world to the plight of allegedly downtrodden Croatia within Yugoslavia, and when the plane landed at a New York airport their actions resulted in the death of one American police officer and the wounding of another. These lovers and murderers did their time—Julienne's sentence, shorter, Zvonko's, longer. For some fifty years both of them have been Croatian heroes; Zvonko died recently, while Julienne is still alive. Julienne, who has meanwhile become a Croatian author, has written about her life with famous Tajko (*Lovers and Madmen*) and has made a documentary (also about her life with Tajko), with the electrifying title: *Your Blood and Mine*. Julienne lives the writer's dream in a villa on the Adriatic that was built for her by the Croatian Army in recognition of all she has done for Croatia.

General Ante Gotovina, the greatest Croat of all, a national icon, had been a professional hit man, trained by the Foreign Legion, before driving some quarter of a million Serbs "peaceably" from Croatia during Operation Storm in the 1990s. General Gotovina has now dedicated himself to aquafarming tuna—and to art. Purportedly, General Gotovina paints. "I always wanted to be a painter," he announced to reporters.

Another man, a Croatian politician and businessman, put in an appearance at the opening of an art show of his work. He had cultivated his artistic talent while serving out his prison sentence for vehicular manslaughter: he killed an innocent, elderly woman from Hungary. Upon his release from prison, the exhibition of his artwork had been organized by friends and admirers to bolster his artistic and personal morale.

Yet another man, one of Croatia's former prime ministers, in prison for grievous malfeasance, had expressed his artistic leanings even before setting out on his political and criminal career. He wrote poems, studied literature, and worked for a time as an editor in a publishing house. And then—once he'd embarked on his political career and found ways to pocket vast sums of money—he gave himself over to collecting art.

And another Croatian "politician and businessman" pocketed several big billions and little millions. After his arrest the TV cameras toured his property. It was no less lavish than the estate of former Ukrainian president Viktor Yanukovych: the same interiors, exteriors, the same catacombs overflowing with "artworks," the same stuffed bears and antlers mounted on the walls.

All these people and many others have been busily penning memoirs. Composing music. Painting. And the media updates us on their "artistic inclinations." Stars and starlets do whatever they can pull off to monopolize the media with their amorous confessions, pornographic reminiscences, criminals with their memoirs, generals with jottings about their wartime valor, politicians with autobiographical sketches about their part in creating the glorious Croatian state, housewives with advice on how to design a garden . . . All of them begin their books with slobber about how they're writing for the sake of their grandchildren, although for their grandchildren's and everyone else's sake it would have been better if they hadn't.

Vojislav Šešelj, the notorious Serbian criminal who was released from the Hague Tribunal, is a fine example of this creative criminal torrent on the Serbian side. Šešelj used his time in Hague incarceration as if it were a leisurely stay at an art residency and wrote a pile of books (about his personal contribution to the building of the Serbian state) which are longer, page wise, than Haruki Murakami's and Knausgaard's contributions to world literature combined.

And Radovan Karadžić—psychiatrist and poet—was given a life sentence. We can only imagine what splendid works Karadžić will produce for Serbian or Bosnian-Serb literature while living out the remainder of his days in prison.

All of them—as Ratko Mladić put so lyrically—worry only about the legacy they'll leave for their people and their generation. They all know full well that they are "first among equals," as the Croatian murderers convicted of war crimes informed the Croatian government from the prison in The Hague.

All this would be fine. Why not let a thousand flowers bloom? Each of us can be *nourishment for the mind of a child*, as a Croatian amateur poet says in celebration of literature. Murderers and criminals are, however, remarkably ambitious, their appetite is growing, it is not enough for them that they have published *their own* books, have had *their own* solo and group shows, garnered media attention; they want acclaim, they want the society they have bestrewn with *their* artworks to genuflect before them. Front and center at every theater's opening night, at every new show, they pontificate on the aesthetic values of each movie, book, performance. But even that is not enough, they aspire to wield total control over whatever realm of art is inhabited by their hobby. They are more than happy to join committees, editorial boards, councils; they become members of juries, elbow their way onto school curricula, into primers, textbooks, anthologies. Their hunger is insatiable, and they have not been loath to accept academic honors. Up and down Croatia strut ex-truckers, generals, badasses, cutthroats, politicians, swindlers, mayors, and crooks, laureled with fake university diplomas and honorable doctorates.

5.

The email from my friend about the Belgrade TV show at the Book Fair sparked my imagination. Chilled by the nightmare vision of millions of people worldwide from an array of occupations clutching their books, and millions more, adamant that it was only a matter of time before they, too, had their own book in hand, and inspired by the movie *Fifty Shades of Gray*, which I watched along with millions of other earthlings, I decided to put an end to my nightmares. I went off to a store that sold practical merchandise. There I purchased the strongest rope I could find, sturdy iron stakes (as if off to scale a mountain), a drill. The salespeople jollied me into buying it all and as a bonus they threw in adhesive strips. The usually snarky salespeople proved unexpectedly solicitous in my case.

I'd decided to end it all. As far as suicidal practices and strategies go I may be an amateur, but I am well-read. Recent statistics suggest that women who commit suicide no longer rely on pills, nor do they lean toward the good old technique of slitting wrists; instead they tend to embrace the *Bye-bye World!* trajectory of the "male" technique of hanging. This, then, was why a key item on my shopping list was the rope. Only a few months later we learned that hanging is not the preference for men; General Slobodan Praljak, having heard his sentence read out in The Hague, downed a little flask of poison before the "cameras of the world." One might say that his theatrical instinct had the upper hand; he did die. His grimly frozen head and gaping mouth lingered on screen.

So what a surprise it was when, as I was leaving the store with these useful purchases, I ran into my very own crook. How? It's easy: Croatia is a tiny country where everybody knows everybody else, as a person from China once remarked, amazed when he was informed of its size. My crook had attended the same elementary school as I did, this being nothing special. Had I the time and will to do the research, I'd probably learn that I rubbed elbows at school and elsewhere with half of the Croatian parliament. In a country as small as Croatia you may well find yourself at the same sports center as the current minister of agriculture, or splashing in a pool with the minister of health, whether past, future, or present. All in all, the current president of tiny Croatia had neglected to invite my crook to a state reception, to which many other deserving crooks were invited, and this filled him with bleak despair, especially as only a few months earlier he, himself, had been a serious contender for the presidency. Oozing natural-born compassion, I stroked his injured ego with a verbal feather and he agreed to come by for coffee. Would you like to hear who he was? You know perfectly well that such a question is pointless: the same goes for all of them. They rule the newspaper and TV roosts, hold our attention rapt, consume us, but as soon as their moment passes no one can even remember their name or anything about them.

And so it was that my crook settled into an easy chair at my place, and from there embarked on a tawdry and shameless lament about how hard this had been for him, but his chums persuaded him, because he had his own occupation, which he loved . . . Oh? He assumed I would have known, of course, he'd earned his degree as a veterinarian but never worked as one . . . And then the war happened, he enlisted with his chums, the homeland needed defending after all; later he landed in politics, how could he refuse to serve, and along the way started a business, a major one, a chain of butcher stores, although his father-in-law was listed as proprietor on the deed, that's right, Znidaršić, well, well, see? You did know after all! His father-in-law freed him of any obligations so he could devote himself to politics. And his children's education. He was wracking his brains at the moment over which English college he should send his son to. The younger one. His older boy was wrapping up a law degree at Harvard . . .

Yet despite all his many obligations he still found time for his beloved pastime, writing. Didn't I know? Well how could I, we hadn't seen each other since our school days, yes, and frankly, even he hadn't known till recently that he had the gift, his wife prevailed upon him to try, this writing thing was a real revelation,

I would definitely find what he'd written interesting, he'd heard, heh heh, heh—that I, too, have been wont to dabble, and that my dabbles have enjoyed a modicum of international renown . . . He'd published a book or two, memoirs, they'd been well-received, locally of course, he had no greater ambitions, he was writing so his grandchildren would remember him . . . It was all over the media, oh yes! That's why he was so startled I hadn't heard!

I'll cut to the chase: the rope I'd planned to use to string myself up I used instead to bind the wrists and ankles of my crook. The adhesive strips came in handy; at one moment my crook got to talking so volubly that it was as if all the TV cameras of the world were trained on him. I had to shut him up somehow . . .

Suicide no longer has any appeal for me. My kidnapee, the crook, has hunkered down with me in a bizarre coexistence. I confiscated his credit cards; this felt like a fair decision. We are currently spending the money he was saving for his children's education. Bye-bye, Oxford, bye-bye Cambridge! But I believe he's most rankled by his family's utter indifference to his disappearance, and the media, to his shock and surprise, made no effort to stir up a fuss. This lack of interest on the part of the media, which has so unnerved my crook—the ill-starred presidential candidate— can be explained by the recent upsurge in similar cases; all the Croatian crooks have been siphoning off funds to overseas bank accounts, declaring bankruptcy, and then disappearing. Everyone else, of course, knows where to find them, but nobody cares, the money is gone and will never be recovered. The future, after all, is in the hands of the next round of crooks.

And something else. I can assert now with confidence that physical pain spurs one's capacity for memorization. The classic educational methods appear to be the most efficient: hunger, humiliation, the switch. Meanwhile I expanded my hoard of props thanks to the possibilities offered by online shopping, encouraged by the agile author of *Fifty Shades of Gray*. I procured handcuffs, a whip, and the ever-popular nipple clamps. These, however, I tossed, because I noticed that my crook was beginning to enjoy them.

There are moments when I feel that the author of *Fifty Shades of Gray* is truly a political and artistic beacon, like Maxim Gorky was in his day, for she has shed light on global relations by showing how rooted they are in exploitation of all kinds, in sadomasochistic relations. Guided by this emancipation idea, I flog my crook with glee . . . So, you want to be a writer, do you, Mr. Slime in Human Form? Compare yourself to Andrić, do you?! Out to outdo Krleža, you ignorant asshole? Well if that's so, let's get a move on, tough guy, set the gray matter humming, time to learn Krleža's *Ballads of Petrica Kerempuh* by heart! Domestic literature too limiting? No problem. Let's get a move on with Shakespeare, and if you survive that, you lousiest of lice, then on we'll go . . .

It remains to be seen whether there will be an upside to my literary-political activism. People ought to learn how to withstand the siren call of artistic amateurism, especially as global praxis has shown that mankind is moving in the opposite direction. Even Bill Clinton hasn't been able to resist. He has announced the publication of his first novel, a partita for four hands with James Patterson. The title: *The President Is Missing*.

December 2017

Zelenko and His Missus

We buy our clothes and all our goods
At the co-op in the neighborhood!

Primer, 1957

No need to wait for the statistical data to shed light on the lives of migrants. The practiced eye catches and organizes the data far faster. This data is not objective, but objective data is not what we're after anyway; we don't know what we'd do with it if we had it. Aside from being useless, it's also boring. The countries that complain the most about the migrants, or those who boast the most about their hospitality, seldom allow in more than five percent of the "intruders." When the hue and cry is at its worst, when protests make it sound as if the percentage of migrants within the general population must be reaching 50%, then you can be sure it never tops 5%. And besides, Croatia has also effectively reduced its population of Serbs, its Croatian Serbs, from the 12% they comprised before the war to slightly below 4%. Yet Croatia still behaves as if the percentage of Serbs is dizzying. Whenever Serbs are mentioned, Croats reach for their phantom limb to scratch it. In political medicine this is known as the syndrome of Croatian-minority phantom limb.

Although Amsterdam boasts that there are more than a hundred ethnicities living there, and although half of Amsterdam's residents are "emigrants," their presence in the city center is scarcely visible. Everything apart from the majority is relegated to the periphery.

I heard stories about Zelenko for years from my compatriots in Amsterdam. We were just at Zelenko's, we bought *our* wine, you should go to Zelenko's, he has *our* relishes and sausages, *sujuk*, and olive oil. And our *Cedevita* powdered orange drink! It turned out that for all these years they'd been trekking to Zelenko, I was the only one who hadn't been. And no matter how often I asked my friends to take me there, they never did. Too far, we'd need a car, we'll have to show you where, and nobody can find it on their own. So the years passed, and I never went to Zelenko's. Until recently when an efficient friend of mine came by, picked me up in her car, and drove me to the eastern reaches of Amsterdam. There, by the terminal for a flock of Amsterdam tourist buses, is where to find Zelenko.

My friend rang the doorbell. Nobody came. She rang again.

We shifted from foot to foot by the door, and then my friend said, disappointed:

"I guess they aren't open today."

We'd already made our peace with this and had turned to go, when the door cracked reluctantly open. The bleary face of a disheveled, puffy woman appeared at the door; she was brushing crumbs from her chin.

"We are in the middle of breakfast!" she said gloomily.

And the door closed.

We waited. The day was sunny. We ambled around by the door and chatted. Then it opened again. There was nobody there this time. In we went. The warehouse wasn't large, in fact it was much more modest than I'd expected, after the briefings and enthusiastic accounts from my compatriots. The merchandise was set out in an orderly fashion, but there were no prices displayed. My friend and I perked right up. There were chocolate-covered *Domaćica* cookies for sale, which we remembered from the old Yugoslav days (they used to melt so yummily on the sunny Adriatic beaches), a variety of smoked-meat products, from *kulen* to *kulenova seka* (what a cute name, *kulen's* little sister!) which, to be frank, nobody eats anymore, to *our* canned beans, *our* ajvar relish and jams, *our* mineral water, and *our* wines. Everything was likely to be outrageously priced in comparison to the similar, or even *identical* merchandise at the Bulgarian and Turkish stores, but here we felt it was *ours* (although in the Turkish stores everything is also *ours*, such as Minas coffee, which was always Turkish, it's just that we, Yugoslavs, adopted it as *our* own). I know how myths about products travel, I have friends, *ours*, scattered all over the world, and I inspect their kitchen drawers in Berlin, New York, Los Angeles, and London, certain I'll find our Kafetin tablets in golden foil packets, the best pills in the world for treating headaches. Nothing treats a headache like *our* Kafetin.

My friend and I filled our baskets. I asked about the prices and
the potato-like woman shot off the numbers as if from a cannon.

"I knew it," she muttered.

"Sorry?" asked my friend.

The woman mumbled something more.

"Ma'am has something upset you?" asked my friend kindly.

"Soon as she walked in here, I knew she wouldn't buy anything," muttered the potato-woman to herself. *She* was me.

We repeated our questions, but the woman shrugged us off
and went to another room. We went over to the cash register,
where the famous Zelenko himself was waiting. His appearance
reminded me of Slavonian smoked sausage.

"Is your wife mad at us for some reason?" cooed my friend, trying to find out why the sudden intolerance from Zelenko's missus.

"Well, you know how it is, we have a lot on our hands," muttered Zelenko.

"I don't understand," I joined the conversation.

"Well you know, people come by, they buy stuff, sometimes
there's a whole crowd, they fill up their shopping baskets, pay up,
and go."

"And? As far as I can see there's nobody here now," I said, still
not catching on.

"It's just that we aren't used to . . . And besides, you asked
about the prices!" now the old man was starting to grouse.

"Why don't you display them?"

"That's not the way we do things. We're not used to it. We
have our hands full, and not . . ." scowled the old man.

"But the place is empty!"

"That's not how we do things. We're not used to it . . ." he kept
up his mantra.

I have to assume that Mr. Zelenko had never, even once in his life, looked anybody in the eyes, even his own missus, because while I was watching him, I had the impression that his eyes had no pupils. I left my full shopping basket on the counter and walked out. My friend did the same. The door slammed behind us.

Why am I bugging my reader and describing at such length this entirely unremarkable and uninteresting episode of daily Amsterdam life? Because the episode so precisely describes the relationship between the individual and government, between citizens and their states of Croatia, Bosnia, Serbia, Macedonia, and because it describes marital, friendship-based, business, familial, and every other kind of relationship. Zelenko and his bleary-eyed missus represent a pattern. How? First of all, they are our democratic government. The government is clearly dubious, and if not outright illegal then surely it's semi-illegal. And just so we don't forget, their enterprise is known as a *warehouse*, not a *store*. Our semi-states are run in a similar way. My friend says that Zelenko has a son. It is easy to imagine that Zelenko and his potato-wife merely serve as a front for other illegal activity. We, the citizens of Zelenko-Land, know nothing about this. Yet we, the citizens of Zelenko-Land elected them, Zelenko and his missus, to office to represent us. Zelenko is always a curmudgeon, and his missus is always bleary, they eat breakfast all morning till noon, and when they converse with members of their community they brush the crumbs off their chins like flies. We are expected to be quick when we buy from them, without asking for the price, to leave our money and get out of there, and be grateful that people like Zelenko and his missus exist at all. They feed us, not we them, they bring us joy, not we them. Only in their warehouse do we feel completely *ourselves*, buying something of *ours*, and exchanging a few grunting half-sounds with them. Although we know that *ours* isn't ours, the ajvar relish isn't *ours* from Serbia, but *ours* from Turkey, that the cookies are actually Bulgarian, but just repackaged as *ours*, that the rahatluk is not *ours* from Bosnia, but *ours* from Turkey—we are there buying *ours*.

And then the question: where does this masochism of *ours* come from, this deep scorn for ourselves? Why do we keep going to Zelenko and his missus even though we know we are overpaying *our* people, and their business is illegal, and we, therefore, are their hostages? They are selling garbage, bribing us with the idea that this garbage is *ours*, and we chew on the *ourness* as if it were a long prison sentence, because this *ourness* is nothing short of a prison sentence. And why don't we give smoked-meat Zelenko and his bleary-eyed missus the finger? What are we afraid of?

Zelenko and his missus are more than just themselves, and this is why we're fascinated by them. We gaze at them as if into a mirror, seeking our own reflection. Zelenko and his missus humiliate others, they are thrilled by the chance to put others down, slam the door, snarl, be rude, brazenly bare their vulgarity, all this so excites them that Mrs. Zelenko pulls down her panties, and Daddy Zelenko his trousers—he presses up against his missus in a corner of the warehouse, among the canned beans and smoked pork tenderloin, *world's finest*. They huff and puff with satisfaction, then they straighten up, open the door and screech: *We're in the middle of breakfast*! This is how they made their son, amid the smoked pork and beans, to mark him with a permanent stamp, so their son, God forbid, won't take after the Dutch. And we, the customers, we too are, of course, the same, we are no better, give us a little authority, any sort of authority, and we'll instantly become Zelenko and his missus. *We're in the middle of breakfast,* screech the metallic voices of the electricians, drivers of large trucks, editors in publishing houses, journalists, writers, hairdressers, teachers, professors, physicians, politicians, ministers of this or that, *it's just that we're not used to it,* they grumble. That's what we're like, we are not emancipated from the adopted model, only this model excites us so we stomp on someone, someone stomps on us, we can tread on someone's bunions, someone treads on ours, we spit in somebody's soup, somebody spits in ours, we insult someone, someone insults us . . .

"If they were a little out of sorts, you should cut them some slack," says my friend in a conciliatory tone. "Zelenko and his missus aren't well . . ."

"Really?"

"I don't know, but I heard from *ours* that they're not doing well. And they have problems with their son."

"Health related?"

"No, something criminal," she says, and adds: "Poor folks."

"Ah yes, poor them . . ."

My friend and I went off to a Turkish store in seek of consolation. There we found a large selection of *our* ajvar relishes, frozen spinach pies, bureks, and jams . . .

"Every once in a while a person feels the need," she said while we sat in a cozy Amsterdam café, sipping our cappuccinos. "What's *ours* is, after all, *ours.*"

We burst out in heartfelt laughter. Down my cheeks and hers slid a few mirthful tears . . .

May 2015

The Little Guys
and "Gypsy Fortune"

Come down, God, to earth
And have mercy on us people

From the heavens you can't see
What I see on earth

Come down, God, to earth
And have mercy on us people

Down here on earth it's not
Like up there in heaven

Come down, God, to earth
And have mercy on us people

Up in heaven there's no
Drifting like here

Come down, God, to earth
And have mercy on us people

When you get tired, have a beer
And back up you go.

(From *Ciganska poezija [Roma Verse]* by R. Uhlik and V. Radičević)

1.

The "little guy," the "average Joe," the "common man," the "nameless," the "statistic," never, throughout the long history of mankind, has had the chance to be the center of attention. Just as there are few public monuments dedicated to the potato[7] or rice (though it's the potato and rice—not the military leaders—that have fed mankind), there are no monuments glorifying the *little guy*. The little guy has been an extra in historical extravaganzas, he has given his small life for grand victories, kings, emperors, and leaders; he built his anonymous bones into the celebrated pyramids and our "glorious future." The little guys died en masse, anonymous, while on the historical surface the bosses, the big names remained. Were the big names truly great? This is a question for dominant-male historical evaluation: one invented the light bulb, another murdered hundreds of thousands of people, one invented the washing machine, another, the gas chamber. The little guy was left nameless and condemned to be an everlasting statistic. And the uprisings and revolutions did not awaken in the little guy the awareness of *man, how proud it sounds*, nor did Maxim Gorky, the author of that slogan, nor did democracy. It was the digital revolution: something Communism only dreamed of but technology realized. Technology has empowered him, our former statistic, to finally take center stage. Did not he, this worm in human form, also come into the world to leave his mark?! And sure enough, the little guys have raced to leave their mark, developing in the process voracious appetites: some of them strip naked

---

7 A monument to the potato was raised in Belica, a little town in Međimurje, where the majority of the population are potato farmers (2007), and there is another in the Novgorod region of Russia. And Boston has its popular Potato Shed Memorial.

and bare their posterior, others their genitalia, some sing, others write, some dance, others paint, while some are multiplexes and do all of this at once. The little guy has finally conquered the media. He gives public talks as, for instance, does Borna Rajić, a Croatian starlet, apparently ageless. She is the ex-wife of Luka Rajić, a former truckdriver for the Dukat Dairy who is now an elite member of the 300 richest people in Switzerland (he, too, was a little guy, Croatian, who overnight realized his dream and became a multimillionaire with a Swiss address). Borna dedicates her vlogs to interpreting Albert Einstein, though she's never earned a degree in physics or mathematics. One of the first Croatian influencers, she has embraced the slogan: *man, how proud it sounds.* The little guy has embraced the chance, through technology, to realize all his potential.

This *little guy* has created his own encyclopedias, accessible to everyone, his alternative forums, his video pieces and his video art, his online newspapers, his values, his pop stars—everything all his own. The result of this colossal self-liberation is mail (electronic), which no longer serves so the senders can ask you how you are, but to foist on you how they are, the successes they've achieved, what new subjects they've written, painted, photographed, and given talks about, where they've been, and what they've participated in. The *little guys* have everything the former *big guys* had, their own media, blogs, websites, Facebook pages, Twitter accounts, selfies, Instagram, text messages. The *big guy* is trying ever harder to catch the *little guy*'s attention. And those who truly rule the world can finally kick back and rest, because today every Narcissus on planet Earth can afford a mirror. Spurred by the urge to be heard, seen, and remembered, the *little guy* is ready for everything except a return to anonymity. Once awoken, the hunger is so powerful that nothing will satisfy it. Communism, which promised years ago that people in the future would be able to engage in free activities, did not keep its promise, but technology has. It's thanks to digital technology, not Marx, that the *little guy* has ventured with one foot into Communism. Technology has made it possible for power to finally pass into the hands of the people. The carnival, which in the pre-digital era was allowed only once a year, and served as a way to ridicule the institutions of power, the priests, emperors, kings, dictators, and politicians—is now a constant in our digital age. The difference lies in the fact that today's carnival-goer seldom skewers the powers that be, he's far too infatuated with his own image to do that. Participants in the carnival in the pre-digital ages wore masks, today everyone does their level best to show his own face.

And if somebody thinks that ours is a vulgar time, they're right. There's no reason to feel embarrassed about saying so out loud because nobody listens to what we're saying anyway. In our digital age, life itself is lived as a carnival, and that's why there's no respite while the carnival goes on. Exhausted people leer from their selfies and for the millionth time they repeat their joy. They are *having fun*, really having a blast, the only thing is there's nobody around who'd dare turn down the blaring music, turn off the spigot for the drinks, and refuse to take part in the self-oblivion. And all the world looks like a beach party, bare-naked bodies chanting Gorky's *man, how proud it sounds*, that everything is cool, couldn't be cooler, the party will last till the liberated bodies are stilled by that inevitable shovelful of dirt.

2.

And while we're on the subject, *Nederlands Uitvaart Museum Tot Zover*, the Amsterdam National Museum of Funeral History, is an unusual place where the visitor can learn about the funereal practices of various peoples. There I learned that the Surinamese put a little bag in the coffin with the deceased, and, in it, a piece of candy, a coin, and a length of white thread; the Chinese put in food, a wok for preparing the food, a transistor, and so forth, all of them made of paper. The Chinese, apparently, favor cremation.

What brought me to the museum, however, was a June 2015 exhibition dedicated to the suicides brought on by the 2008–2013 financial crisis. Aside from photographs on a wall of shame, the show was filled with copies of a single book. The book is reminiscent of a monumental dictionary, its cloth cover is red and black, and the black pages are printed with white letters. *The Complete Lexicon of Crisis-Related Suicides 2008–2013* is the work of graphic designer Richard Sluijs. It is 712 pages long and weighs some four pounds. Each page is designed like a death notice, a paper tombstone with the name of the suicide victim, the date when the person killed themselves, what provoked them to take their life, and how they did it. The book grew into a paper burial ground, on the left, drawn with white lines, are the gravesite, name, age, nationality, and a symbol for the way the person took his life, on the right is the death notice with explanation. Sluijs designed symbols for jumping, hanging, gunshot, suffocation, overdose (medications, drugs, etc.), knife, poison, drowning, vehicular impact, self-immolation, explosion, and "method unknown." The book states that this is only Volume One; the author wishes to make it clear that the book does not include every single suicide that happened the world over after the financial crisis, nor are the victims fully commemorated on its pages. It's merely drawing attention to this frightening trend. In his introduction, Sluijs provides shocking numbers for the upsurge in suicides due to the recession in many countries. Equally horrifying is the fact that for every "successful" suicide there have been twenty failed attempts. The book serves as a cemetery with some six hundred graves. Here lies Franco D'Argenio (58), a forestry worker from Campania in Italy, who committed suicide by drowning in a water tank after he wasn't paid for seventeen months. Here lies Parang Tanna (34) and his pregnant wife Neha. Parang Tanna first suffocated his wife with a pillow and then hanged himself, after realizing he would not be able to support himself and his family. Here also lies Filipo Arena (30) from the town of Mazara del Vallo, Italy, unemployed, condemned to live with his retired parents . . . And so on and so forth . . .

Richard Sluijs's book will not become a bestseller. It speaks about *little guys* who were and continue to be devastated by the financial crisis, about people whose deaths no longer touch anybody. There are many victims, many more than the author of the book—who is not a sociologist, statistician, economist, or anthropologist, but a graphic designer with a sensitive heart—could possibly collect. And when the victims are many, there's no place for them in human hearts of average emotional capacity. It bears remembering that in this society of ours, rooted in an overweening happiness, empathy has been jettisoned. Everyone is preoccupied with their own life, their own little existence. And as long as people stare obsessively at their reflection on the smooth screen, there will be no room for the lives of others, there is simply no room.

3.

Should visitors stretch their legs only a few steps beyond the museum, located right next to the entrance to the cemetery, they'll come across row upon row of strange and unusually lavish tombs. This is where the Amsterdam Roma with Serbian first and last names are buried. It would seem that cemetery officials everywhere are corruptible: the Serbian Roma at the Amsterdam cemetery managed to secure for themselves front-row placement and founded a preeminent colony for their dead. Roma have to die to be considered first-class citizens. Roma are wanderer-travelers, they settle down only when their bones settle, they find their real home only when they die, this must be why they like having tombs that are much fancier than the average Amsterdam apartment. The tombs are built of the finest marble, some are even wired for electric power, though the cemetery authorities do not allow the lighting of tombs. Many of them have built-in marble benches with marble seats so visitors can rest. Some tombs have gilded ornaments, and the most ostentatious boast the *President* brand name. Photographs of the deceased are engraved on the tombstone, some show scenes from the everyday life of the deceased—a husband and wife sipping coffee in the shade of a tree or stepping into a deluxe white Mercedes[8]. Some choose photographs from

---

8 "Gypsy fortune" refers to an old Mercedes model (the 123, I think), a status symbol for generations of guest workers as the crowning achievement of their time spent working in Germany, Switzerland . . . One of the most common taxis used in Serbia until recently because of its characteristics, which allowed it to run for two million kilometers without a hitch on water, oil, and gasoline. It is used as a limousine in

their wedding when they were young and good-looking, some add favorite scenes on which they'll rest their eyes for all eternity— such as a herd of white horses. And, look, Roma who have never been integrated anywhere have become a symbol of integration in their death: many visitors to the cemetery stop by the tombs and photograph them. In this mournful spot there is a certain farcical justice, their graveside is a "fuck you" to the civilization of money, *our* civilization. Up yours, declare the deceased to you, this is *your* culture, we're merely imitating it, this is *your* kitsch, and we are only glorifying it, money and success are *your* values, which are, even for the Roma who choose to make the effort, a snap. The visitors for whom the view of the tombs offers a thrill of superiority (What gauche barbarians! What kitsch! What tons of pointlessly wasted money!) take pictures of the graves with ironic sneers, never guess that the phantoms of the buried Roma are giving them the finger from the beyond.

"Gypsy happiness" lies not here, but elsewhere. I often reread, always with great joy, *Lord, Turn Me into an Ant*, an anthology of Roma fairy tales from Kosovo and Metohija. In these tales, poor people with good hearts master useful skills. Forest, bow down, they say, and look, down bows the forest! In these tales, valiant heroes turn into ravens and ants and they're given the gift of oil lamps from which ducats drop when they're rubbed. In these tales, when water is poured over virtuous maidens, gold coins splash like rain; when maidens weep, pearls course down their cheeks; and carnations tumble from their lips when they

---

Roma weddings, which may be where the name comes from.

Entry in Vukajlija, an unofficial online dictionary of Serbian colloquial usage

smile. And when a comb is thrown to the ground, from it grows a thicket; from a mirror comes a lake; and watermelons rolling down from the sky speak in human tongues . . . What can we say to this except that compared to such flights of Roma fancy, contemporary technology seems stultifyingly inferior. And that is why we're closing this piece with an ending typical of Roma tales. This ending brings a prayer that "gypsy fortune," whatever that means, stays on the Roma side. *There malice—here goodness! There pennies—here biscuits! There villains—here kind souls!*

August 2015

L'ecriture Masculine

"Judge," she said to him, "what's going to happen to the whores?"
Osmolovsky raised his eyes, his face covered in rippled light.
"They will no longer exist."
"Won't the whores be allowed to earn a living?"
"They will," the judge said. "But in a different, better way."

Isaac Babel, "Gapa Guzhva"

1.

Nobody in the history of literature was capable of capturing the entire universe (syphilis & stars!) on a mere five pages of text like Isaac Babel. Although it wasn't designed to be this, Babel's story "The Sin of Jesus" could be a feminist fable, an anti-fairy tale, a women's manifesto, if it weren't, first and foremost, a literary jewel. "The Sin of Jesus" is a story about Arina, a maid at the Hotel Madrid & Louvre, who is pregnant yet again by Seryoga, a hotel janitor; the year before she gave birth to Seryoga's twin girls. And Seryoga, like all other men, is not of much use, especially as he has been recruited to serve for four years in the army. Arina goes to Jesus Christ to have a little chat, she tells him what is troubling her, this is how things stand, Jesus Christ, I'm pregnant, and "working in a hotel, your skirt is hitched up more often than not," so what can I do . . . At this Jesus Christ remembers that an angel by the name of Alfred is hanging around up in heaven, "I'll give you, virginal sinner, Alfred the Angel to be your husband for four years, and he will be your prayer, your protector, and you can have your fun with him," suggests Jesus. Arina thanks the Lord, brings the angel home, prepares a lavish dinner, buys vodka, and the two of them, Alfred and Arina, get drunk. Arina takes the angel's wings off before they go to bed, just as Jesus Christ has told her to, and then they lie down. Overjoyed to be sleeping with an angel, drunken Arina with her six-month belly lies on Alfred and, inadvertently, smothers him. In the morning, awash in tears, she picks up the dead angel and brings him to the Lord. "You smothered my angel, bitch," says Jesus, choking in rage.

"But, sir (. . .) was I to blame for my body swelling? Did I brew the vodka? Am I the one who, lonely and stupid, invented the woman's soul?" says Arina.

And the Lord raises up a mighty wind and with curses he blows Arina back to Hotel Madrid & Louvre. And it is a madhouse there, Seryoga has been recruited and is guzzling booze, the men on whose help Arina was counting, old man Isai Abramich and Trofimich the contractor, are behaving as if they've pulled free of their chains, they call her "big belly," mock her, spit into her soul . . .

Before she gives birth, Arina goes out into the yard, raises her "terrible big belly to the silken skies" and says: "Look, oh Lord, at this belly. Everyone pounds on it like a drum. I understand none of this nor do I want to . . ."

Jesus Christ at that moment grasps the full extent and depth of a woman's torment on Earth, kneels and begs for Arina's forgiveness.

"I will not forgive you, Jesus Christ, I will not!" answers Arina.

2.

In October of 2014, all the newspapers in the world were carrying photographs of American movie actress Renée Zellweger. The press expressed horror at the fact that the actress no longer looked like herself, but like a Hollywood clone. The articles were heartless, as they are toward famously beautiful women who are aging "without dignity," putting on the pounds, wrinkled, and "sagging, like nylons" (the stockings worn before pantyhose), or undergoing plastic surgery that fails to give the desired result. Renée Zellweger had slid into the latter category, and from here on in, unless a miracle happens, she'll stay trapped in this *before–after* circle of hell, along with her colleagues, Meg Ryan and Melanie Griffith. In hell, as in life, the *after* is always worse than the *before*. Only in paradise is the *after* better.

It is hardly a revelation that thanks to technology, the tribes in New Guinea can, if they like, discuss whether Renée Zellweger looks better before or after. Surprising is that even the tribes of New Guinea are willing to discuss this. Why? Because the interest stems mainly from men, and rises out of a secret, sweet inclination toward a particular vandalism aimed at women.

In many parts of ex-Yugoslavia, I often saw posters advertising concerts of local singers. The faces of the female vocalists were regularly defaced by mustaches, the teeth in the smile colored-in black, and the chin bedecked with whiskers. A flying penis winged by under the nose of the pretty singer. This flying penis was supposed to inspire the deepest erotic fantasies of the lovely lady on the poster. But actually—along with the mustache, blackened teeth, and chin whiskers—the flying penis was the sweet erotic fantasy of a man, the anonymous vandal.

The defiling of posters showing women's faces has remained a beloved form of vandalism to this day, and this vandalism is hardly the exclusive property of men from ex-Yugoslav lands. This brand of vandalism is a form of misogyny, and misogyny has no narrowly national character, nor is this disease endemic. Misogyny is a cloaked form of male writing. Vandalism directed at women has its symbolic and concrete forms. In the category of vandalism (until the law begins treating this as a crime) belong: the customs related to mutilating a woman who is unfaithful (burning her face with hydrochloric acid), burying "sinful women" alive, leaving only their head above ground (allegedly, a practice in India), burning, starving, and physically punishing women (in India, Pakistan, Afghanistan, and elsewhere they punish elderly women, widows, this way, who are no longer able to contribute financially to the family), the customs of group rapes of women, clitoridectomy (mutilation of women's sexual organs which, as a rule, is done by women), various forms of physical abuse, sadism, ridicule, humiliation and intimidation, banning abortion, family and marital violence, bullying, obstructing employment, the equal right to work, to earnings, to equal participation in all spheres of professional, political, economic, and cultural life, the use of technological innovations to bully women (the internet, social media, selfies, Instagram), cyberstalking, cyber violence . . . Vandalism is used by misogynists to humiliate and intimidate women, and subject women to men's aesthetic, moral, social, and sexual tastes, to male dominance. Renée Zellweger is merely the freshest victim of the same pattern of intimidation: her experience signals to her that she mustn't age, she mustn't allow herself to become uglier, because otherwise she'll lose all she has: respect, work, the love of her community, her partner, children, money, a secure and respectable life. An intelligent woman will do everything she can to put off the moment when she has to step down from the stage of life into the world behind the stage, down the steps, downward into the underground, into age, the dark, a coffin, nothingness. Men have Viagra—women have plastic surgeons.

3.

Men's writing is invariably in the plural, while women's is in the singular. Men think and say *we*, while women generally say *I*. Men's writing is dominant and authoritative, while women's speaks from a minority position, almost "illegally," antiauthoritarian. Women in their "writing" often speak to men, while men mostly speak to other men. Girls love boys, boys love boys. Women are the most skilled in the language of physical exhibitionism, they have conditioned themselves to that kind of speech because they have always been applauded for it by men.

In every literature there is one writer, or more, who earns this sort of applause. Every literature has its Charlotte Roche. The Dutch version is a woman named Heleen van Royen, author of the novel *The Happy Housewife*, a huge hit in the Netherlands. This attractive writer has been exciting the attention of TV cameras wherever she has gone, her books are bestsellers, and the Dutch cultural scene, using the term "neo-feminism" as a literary/evaluative alibi, is more prepared to canonize Heleen van Royen than a more serious, quieter woman author. Why? Because literary canonization is done by men, and also because Heleen van Royen is in no way their rival. This is how porn, thanks to male selection and evaluation, accrues literary value. The Museum of Literature in The Hague purchased Heleen van Royen's archive and organized the exhibit, *Heleen van Royen: Selfmade*, where the author exhibited her selfies, vibrators, lingerie, and other similar objects of artistic value. Heleen van Royen provoked attention when she photographed her vagina, from which hung the string of a tampon, and critics declared this an "act of courage" and "pushing the limits" in discovering female physicality. The author moved television audiences by declaring, about the tampon-selfie, that every menstruation is cause for celebration—because it fends off menopause for yet another month. About another image, "Selfie with Sperm," Heleen van Royen sparked a lively discussion about whether the unusual droplets in the author's hair merely looked like sperm or actually were sperm, which the author claimed they were, saying she loved artistic work with sperm. The author published a lavish monograph of her selfies. Prints of the selfies, two hundred of them, are for sale online, over Catawiki, where each commands a high price.

4.

It's as if women, from the moment they're born, adopt the dangerous meme that the only thing they have to offer, the only thing they can sell, is their body. Renée Zellweger, desiring to be younger and prettier, changed her appearance until she was unrecognizable. Heleen van Royen sends selfies out into the world: a tampon in her vagina and sperm in her hair, which are, in her opinion, the only relevant proof that she's alive. Lena Dunham, a young New York actress, director, and screenwriter, is the director of *Tiny Furniture*, an excellent short film, the *Girls* HBO series, and *Not That Kind of Girl*, a book. Charming, witty, young, emancipated, candid, Lena Dunham is well aware of the privileged social position (New York, both parents successful artists, a good education, affluent, white, famous) from which she speaks. Yet regardless of how emancipated she may be, regardless of the way she waltzes, bare-bottomed, around on the screen as if this were the most natural thing to do in the world, Lena Dunham and her friends have, it seems, the same problem and same treatment from men as their mothers did. Dunham, who insists on the fact that she is liked just the way she is, realizes that full emancipation is a particularly challenging task. She remarks that she is sorry for being who she is, for existing, and many young women have this feeling who apologize for existing, for what they've done, even when they haven't done anything.

Dunham has zeroed in on women's low self-esteem, their self-harming, self-humiliation, and self-loathing, the way women are always apologizing for the fact that they even exist. This is the acupuncture point that men either consciously or unconsciously stimulate so they can hold women under their sway. And here we are, we have approached hidden, well-camouflaged fascism: only beautiful, slender, white women, "Aryans," the ones who correspond to the generally acceptable standard, have the right to life and procreation. How far from this understanding is the move Renée Zellweger made (and with her, many other actresses and many other women and anonymous women, including a young Bosnian woman who has undergone several operations already to make herself look more like Angelina Jolie)? And doesn't her "fall" confirm that she was right?

5.

"He was still looking at her crotch, that tiny little area that, with admirable economy of space, provides for four sovereign functions: arousal, copulation, procreation, urination. He gazed a long while at that sad place with its spell broken, and was gripped by an immense, immense sadness." So contemplates, with melancholy, the misogynist hero of Milan Kundera's novel *Ignorance*.

A good Croatian journalist who has been writing a regular column in the local papers for the last twenty years, a cultural opinion-maker, reviewed the Nancy Kates movie *Regarding Susan Sontag*. The review focuses more on Susan Sontag, in fact, than on the movie. Mentioning Sontag's book *On Photography*, the Croatian journalist says that "although there are better books on the subject," *On Photography* enjoys cult status. He goes on to say that Sontag dabbled in "this and that," that she was not " a successful writer, or, in the true sense, a journalist, and she didn't write as a scholar, but in the peripheral zone of all three of these professional realms she managed to impose herself with her essays as an essential opinion-maker in a society with a strong preference for expert-specialists, not for sharp-eyed jacks-of-all-trades." Sontag used her portrait photographs, in his opinion, to "construct her own public persona," she "controlled her own visual image." The critic avers that in photographs, one can see "her narcissistic pleasure at posing," the photographs "show a person who lets it be known that she is posing for eternity."

We might imagine the situation this way, too: in a small provincial town, which has no opera house, posters announce the concert of a world-famous diva. The provincial opera lover takes out a big black marker and draws on the poster a beard, mustache, blackens the diva's teeth, and adds the sketch of the flying penis. He does this furtively, like our journalist with his jabs at Susan Sontag. Because who will, for God's sake, ever learn of his petty act of defilement in the Croatian daily papers! Something like this will only be known to the women reading the article in Croatian, potentially there are two million of them, hence one half of the total population of Croatia. If it ever should occur to a woman to dabble in "this and that" (unlike journalists who deal seriously with "something"), expose "her narcissistic pleasure at posing," and "impose herself as an essential opinion-maker," and doing this, God forbid, in New York—such a "jack-of-all-trades" should know what was waiting for her in little, but well-informed Croatia.

In the culture zone from which I took this example, misogyny functions a little like radiation. It is invisible and not a single person is spared by it. People do not die from this radiation, they live out their lives without realizing how bad it is. Even the finest succumb to this brand of radiation illness, like the Croatian journalist quoted above. Misogyny is ubiquitous, in the nursery schools, elementary and secondary schools, universities, in textbooks, novels, even scholarly books, in the newspapers, on television, in the movies, in everyday life, in the family, church, politics, culture, simply everywhere. Perhaps this is why the local spokespeople for women's rights are silent; they can predict in advance the outcome of any confrontation so they retreat into their invisible corners and putter along on modest internet portals, followed by a dozen women members, in their little NGOs and modest programs, in academic communications—conferences and essay collections—where the same participants circulate for years, convinced that they are undertaking something of earth-shattering importance.

6.

The dance is called the *horon*, a word related to the word *korus* (*chorus*). Men dance the *horon* in northern Turkey, on the Black Sea shores. The *horon* is much like a Georgian dance known as the *horumi*; there are many iterations. The specific movements—the jiggling of the upper part of the body like the wobbling breasts of belly dancers—are, apparently, inspired by the way the *hamsi*, a species of Black Sea fish, moves.

Here, however, we are interested in an amateur video that has been on YouTube for several years. The video shows four men at the older end of middle age dancing the *horon*. The video was made at a village wedding (possibly in northern Turkey) and has the jocular title: *Dirty Dancing*. The amateur camera is focused on the four dancers and it is only after a good two minutes that we see the bride. She is in a long white wedding dress, planted on a chair in the mud of the village yard, watching the dance performance with indifference. The bride is surrounded by women: the elder women are wearing head scarves and baggy trousers. They all watch the four men dance with identical expressions—something like bottled-up misery—and now it's certain that they will carry that expression with them to the grave.

The beginning of the dance is poignant, this is the moment when these grown men grab each other by the hand like boys and, moved by the music blaring from unseen speakers, begin their temperamental dance. They shimmy their shoulders and chests, wag their bottoms like sea lions, then kick like rearing horses, then slow their movements and begin inching along with little steps in a circle, until, at one moment they kick again. One of them takes out a pistol and fires off shots into the air, then something gets in his eye, the man next to him in the line of dancers takes a handkerchief from his pocket and gingerly wipes the man's eye. The expressions on their faces suggest the injury is not serious and all four of them continue, unperturbed, with their dance. Then the second takes out a gun and fires it into the air, then the third does the same, and shortly after that, the fourth. On the face of the fourth there are grimaces of dissatisfaction, as if he is a little disappointed that his shooting wasn't loud enough or appreciated.

On they dance, holding hands, elderly, potbellied boys, they keep moving, they dance as if in a trance, time has stopped, they fire off their guns into the sky above their heads, they aren't shooting to outdo one another, their shots are like love messages to each other. The aging boys spin their rumps, shimmy their shoulders, rear up, leaving behind them in the air foggy plumes of smoke.

7.

New products have appeared on the New Year's Eve fireworks market, with a much louder bang than was heard in earlier years. The sound is now reminiscent of the blast of a genuine hand grenade. How do I know? In my Amsterdam neighborhood teenagers and occasionally full-grown men entertain themselves by throwing them. The terror this year began a full two months before the Christmas and New Year's holidays. The blasts woke residents in the apartment buildings. The author or authors of this nocturnal terror remained hidden somewhere in the dark. Male writing. In my thoughts I bitterly acknowledge the male gender, because for centuries now with thunderous noise, shouts, growls, and vocalizing they have forced us to listen. Will this imposition ever stop? Hmm, hard to say, this is about biology: virulent hormones and virulent memes. Human males manifest their presence in all sorts of ways; the only thing they've miscalculated is the timing of mating season, so now they make their noise all the time, ruffle their feathers, pound their chest, prance . . . The fact that they're setting fireworks off two months ahead of schedule suggests a loss of natural rhythm; after all they are urban beings, their biological clocks have long since run out of batteries. Perhaps this is why human females are constantly wiggling their buttocks, bouncing and shaking them, twerking, as if there is no end to the game of simulated mating. Outdoors reverberates one blast, then another. This won't be ending soon, I think. I slip spongy plugs into my ears and crawl back into bed.

October 2014

The Scold's Bridle

... if there's one thing that we know bonds women of all backgrounds, of all political colors, in all kinds of business and profession, it's the classic experience of the failed intervention; you're at a meeting, you make a point, then a short silence follows, and after a few awkward seconds some man picks up where he had just left off: "What I was saying was . . ."

Mary Beard[9]

1.

I was recently on an international panel with two other writers, both men. The moderator was a woman. After we'd read our prepared texts, a question came from the audience to all of us. Before I'd had the chance to open my mouth, the moderator leapt spryly to her feet and whispered to me that I should keep it brief because we had very little time for discussion. My answer took twenty

9 Mary Beard, "The Public Voice of Women." *London Review of Books*, March 20, 2014.

seconds. That was the shortest possible response I could devise. My first colleague spoke for fifteen minutes. The second was somewhat more modest: he spoke only for ten. All the while the moderator never blinked. After the discussion was over she came to apologize. I thought to myself, "Don't worry, sister, we're used to this" and smiled in response. She, too, smiled. We understood each other. This was a *classic experience of the failed intervention* that Mary Beard describes in the opening to this essay. True, this time my wings were clipped by a woman—but it was hardly the first time.

2.

The *scold's bridle* (or *brank's bridle*, or *branks*) is an artifact we now see on display in museums, but from the sixteenth to the nineteenth centuries in Europe (England, Wales, Germany, and Scotland) it was used to punish women who had a lashing, scathing tongue, to punish chatterboxes, gossips, busybodies, yentas, yakety-yaks, nags, harpies, shrews, vixens, quibblers, spitfires, hags, magpies, blabbermouths, prattlers, tattletales, loudmouths, hawkers, fussbudgets, floozies, women with a *tongue as long as a cow's tail*. In Walton-on-Thames one can see a scold's bridle displayed in a church with the inscription: "Chester presents Walton with a bridle to curb women's tongues that talk too idle"; somebody named Chester had apparently lost his fortune because of a gossiping woman, so he donated the iron bridle to the city to stay women's tongues. The first scold's bridle was made in Scotland in 1567; apparently it was still in active use in Bolton-le-Moors, Lancashire, as late as 1856.

3.

The history of the "creative class"—artists, intellectuals, poets, philosophers—is long, dramatic, and almost entirely male, as is, of course, all of history. When we speak of the "public intellectual," we all, men and women alike, automatically imagine men. There is, however, a parallel history that is seldom mentioned or even known: the history of female silence. Mute women, women who have been muzzled by men through the long history of gender relations, have factually and symbolically insured (and still do) the intellectual, political, artistic, ideological, and every other form of *male* production. All this makes women victims, but they, too, bear a serious share of the blame for today's deplorable state of gender inequality.

4.

In her article "The Public Voice of Women," Mary Beard quotes earlier examples of the brutal exclusion of women from the public sphere. Her examples come from the mythology of the classical world and history, such as the story of Lucretia, who was permitted to accuse her rapist publicly but only if her suicide immediately followed the denunciation, the story of Philomela, whose tongue was cut off by her rapist to prevent her from testifying against him, the story of Io, turned by Jupiter into a cow (and cows don't speak, they moo), the story of Echo, forced by Hera, out of jealousy, to give voice only to the words of others, the story of Penelope . . . The songs a street bard was singing drove Penelope to distraction but when she called for a happier subject, Telemachus, her son, stopped her: "Mother, go back up into your quarters, and take up your own work, the loom and the distaff . . . Speech will be the business of men, all men, and of me most of all; for mine is the power in this household."

5.

The sphere of public speech from antiquity to today is ruled by the "law of Telemachus," meaning the holy trinity: the Politician, the Priest, and the Poet, the 3 Ps. Why does the Poet belong there with Priests and Politicians? Because the other two are his smooth-talking "colleagues," masters of hope, a "bright future." The Poet is a "wizard with words," a "nightingale," an "engineer of human souls," but are not, likewise, the Priest and Politician? They, too, hawk illusions; their job is to rule the mob. The Poet is his nation's most venerable maven for public relations. History has been erected on a robust foundation based on the bond among the POLITICIAN, PRIEST, and POET. The POLITICIAN, PRIEST, and POET are the three-headed symbol of traditional national identity, the pillar of governmental authority. Of course, in this holy trinity the POET is the "weakest link." These three Ps have a powerful shadow, the fourth P, the POLICEMAN.

Do women have a voice in church? Little or none. The Bible, the spiritual underpinning of Christian civilization, is profoundly misogynist, much like the holy texts of all the other major religions. Do women have a voice in politics? Yes, when they say what the men in government like to hear. Do they have a voice in the media, in art, in literature? They do, more and more, but generally they are in the "lower sectors": juvenile, pornographic, and genre literature . . . Serious, canonic literature is still reserved for men. The literary canons are studied at school, consequently generations and generations of children, male and female, ingest a "universalist" (male!) outlook on the world.

A contemporary poet genuflects in verse to the Croatian literary canon:

What you've given me, oh Croatia,
are your books.
The verses of your poets
the lines of Hektorović, Ujević, Marun, Gudelj, Simić, Kaštelan.
A vast encyclopedia of sorrow.[10]

To be honest, today's teens in Croatia are reading Harry Potter (if they read at all), or something like it, as do teens the world over. Teenagers have no clue about the names listed here in the "vast encyclopedia of sorrow." In fact two of the names on the list are new even to me. I assume that for the Priest, Politician, and Poet, my (typically female) ignorance is yet another sign that they must push on with building their robust male canon.

6.

The "law of Telemachus" would seem, still, to apply. Perhaps this

---

10 All victories in the political, spiritual, and artistic realms were won by the sons, who fabricated for themselves a desirable mother. In this and many other cases, this mother who bears the famous sons is the homeland, in this case: Croatia. A slightly more modern type of imagined community again is exclusively male. So the Hungarian writer, Szilárd Borbély, who died far too young, said: "We East Europeans, we are all Kafka's sons." Writers in the literary realm are simply not capable of imagining *sisters*!

is because of the overall patriarchization of the societies in Eastern Europe after the fall of Communism; perhaps the reason for this are the new borders, new states, new animosities, the many migrations, the economic crisis, religious conflicts, religious fundamentalism, and the upsurge of nationalism. The church has assumed a pivotal role in all the postcommunist democracies and it has returned the "women's question" to the patriarchal framework. Women had only just found their voices, but now they've gone silent. Never have men perceived of women as equals, as serious conversants anyway, and women haven't yet learned to speak to each other with their "intellectual messages" or to respect each other as collocutors. The "law of Telemachus" is in full force, identical to the classical model of the absence of women from the public, intellectual, creative, political, and media spheres. Women are being sent back to their quarters. We find today's "distaffs and looms" in the nonprofit organizations, in the hushed, hermetic circles of academia, in the women's organizations that tackle "women's subjects" (the trafficking of women, prostitution, the right to an abortion, and so forth). All this difficult and important work remains under the radar. Nobody seems too exercised over the frequent news from India of group rapes of women, or, for example, the million women every year forced into prostitution, but a mocking caricature of a Muslim religious leader that appears in the press is all it takes, and, bingo, the whole world is on its feet.

It should be said that women have not relinquished their strategy of self-humiliation and self-harm in order to adapt themselves to men's expectations. In this sense, Hans Christian Andersen's *The Little Mermaid,* who voluntarily gives up her ability to speak so the prince will like her, and in return is given women's legs, is an unusually precise metaphoric example. A vast industry supports women in their efforts to satisfy men's fantasies and participate successfully in the economy of traditional gender relations. Today their bodies can be shaped and reshaped, their bones, the color of their teeth and eyes, all this can be changed, their organs can be rejuvenated. Meanwhile men are hard at work defending, bolstering, discovering, developing, advancing universal principles. Universal? Sure.

7.

With the fall of Communism, the position of women in the postcommunist societies deteriorated from its earlier status. The communist image of the independent woman who'd been part of the workforce (a priority for post-World-War propaganda because the workforce was short of men and needed women!) has been replaced by the image of the porn star, or the submissive wife who spends her whole life winding herself onto three spools: children, church, kitchen. The resurgence of nationalist ideology in postcommunist countries has had a major impact on the instrumentalization of women. In Croatia (serving here merely as an example of postcommunist transition in the country I know best), some women have become members of the staid Academy of Sciences and Arts, thanks to having a political profile that satisfies their conservative colleagues; some have donned Ustasha uniforms in order to satisfy their Blackshirt brethren and are raising their children to believe that the Jasenovac concentration camp—into which tens of thousands of Jews, Serbs, Romani, and Croatian communists disappeared—was no more than a fiendish communist fabrication. If one counts the number of young women momentarily visible within the ruling Croatian political elite, the right wing would even appear to be more "gender sensitive" than the other political constellations. In general, the right wing in European countries seems to be instrumentalizing women more and more.

The *sponzoruša* (the hottie, or, in Russian slang, the *tyolka*) would seem to be the most sought-after role for a woman in postcommunist societies. Naked young women who crouch on their hands and knees, serving as mute side tables for the cigar ashtrays in Russian steam baths for the filthy rich (something I heard from a reliable source) are just one morbid detail of postcommunist everyday life. Pop stars who are low in the hierarchy of professional qualifications, such as Severina in Croatia and Ceca in Serbia, have become rich and famous national princesses and serve as models for legions of little girls and young women to emulate them throughout the lands of ex-Yugoslavia. However, even highly qualified businesswomen do not pass up the opportunity to parade their traditional medals. A Zagreb physician I know declares on her website that she's married and is the mother of three sons. There's a Catholic crucifix flashing at her throat, signaling that the respected doctor is a Catholic, and, hence, a Croat. Her professional qualifications and achievements hold only third place in her hierarchy of values.

Women can, indeed, succeed in postcommunist societies and realize their right to a public voice. In fact they can even become president. The current president of Croatia, Kolinda Grabar-Kitarović, is a walking instruction manual for "what a woman has to do to become president in a postcommunist society." Kitarović presents herself as a "womanly" woman (she's not a "man in a skirt," she's ethnically "pure" [a Croat], she's religious [Catholic] and socially acceptable [married, mother of two]. Kitarović is a female poltroon, she touts her public respect for all levels of the military, she likes having her picture taken while in military regalia, posing in relaxed scenes with Croatian soldiers. Kitarović publicly declares her sympathy for the CDU, the leading Croatian right-wing party, and political analysts say she is its exponent. When she's asked for her political model, Kitarović says: Margaret Thatcher.

8.

Twelve hundred Croatian high-school seniors were recently surveyed (according to the newspaper *Jutarnji list*), and the responses showed that 75% of them believe the Independent State of Croatia was not, in fact, a fascist puppet state; 40% disapprove of the prosecution of crimes committed during the war between 1991 and 1995; 49% believe homosexuality to be a disease; 43% were serious Catholics and 25% were "fair-weather" believers.[11] Politicians, ministries of culture and education, the governmental bureaucracy, media, journalists, writers, public figures, professors, teachers, the Croatian Academy of Sciences and Arts, schools, university departments, publishers, parents, and the ever-present Catholic church—have all worked diligently and in concert to foster these devastating statistics. Did the men and women of Croatia protest the children's statistical profile? They did not.

---

11 *Jutarnji list*, 1 October 2015.

There are, however, shining examples of women in postcommunist societies who have dared to raise their voice. Their history—after the fall of the Wall, after Yugoslavia collapsed and independent countries were formed out of what had been Yugoslavia—is a brave chronicle of harassment by the media, institutions, police, men, women, politicians, and any number of others. The alternative failed politics of dissent has lasted a quarter century, exactly as long as the successful politics of assent.

9.

In November of last year, parliamentary elections were held in Croatia. A patriotic coalition won, led by the right wing party, CDU. Members of the party celebrated their victory. Men were dropping to their knees and shouting drunken words of gratitude to an invisible god, howling, jiggling, dancing, sweating, sharing slobbery kisses. A video of the celebration went viral. The video shows a squat little man who, in a euphoric frenzy, spreads a Croatian flag out on the ground. A circle of men closes around him, chanting, "Kiss it! Kiss it!" Egged on by the chants of the mob, the man kneels and kisses the flag. The mob chants: "Go! Go! Go!" The man flips over onto his back and at this point looks like a baby squirming on its diaper. Enchanted by the sight, another man flings himself down on top of the first and showers him with kisses. The mob, a little startled by the sight of the two exalted men, starts chanting: "Franjo, Franjo." This necrophiliac emotional twist, their invocation of the dead "father of the nation," Franjo Tuđman, has a Viagra-like effect and the chanting soon spills over into "Croatia, Croatia," a sort of uninterrupted, massive, political orgasm. The squat little man scrambles to his feet, retrieves his flag, and, what do you know, now he's brandishing two: the big cloth flag and a little paper flag on a stick: a "mother" and "daughter" duo. In most Slavic languages the word "homeland" is a noun of the feminine gender, the homeland is the mother, and defending her is men's work. Sexual impotence, homophobia, patriarchalism, Catholicism, a castration complex, and misogyny—all these together fuel the celebratory political orgy.

10.

For years I have been trying to dodge the label "Croatian writer," or "Croatian writer who lives in Amsterdam," though my life experience has confirmed that this sort of tattoo is almost impossible to remove. Why? Because most people use ethnic coordinates when remembering, classifying, defining, and judging others. I'm not comfortable with the label "Croatian writer." Why? Among other things because (had I stayed in Croatia) I would have been constantly exposed to scenes like the ones described above, and I find them difficult to relate to. Consequently, in Croatia (like, indeed, so many other places), the men-writers represent their homeland, state, nation, and national literature, their works harmoniously build the national literary canon. Women-writers are most often victimized by such constellations. The three women who have laid the shaky foundation for the Croatian women's literary canon—Ivana Brlić-Mažuranić, Marija Jurić Zagorka, and Vesna Parun—met tragic ends: the first committed suicide, the second died in penury and neglect, the third played the clown, shunting back and forth between the two options facing her predecessors.

I was recently honored with an international literary prize. The news reached the ears of my exemplary compatriots, though precious few chose to mention it in the media. One critic wrote a review of my most recent book and mentioned the prize as an aside. The reviewer remarked that this "major prize was as much a prize for the oft overlooked Croatian essay" to which "I *owe* (my italics) my voice and form." Did this review, perchance, appear in a right wing rag? Not at all, it was published in a politically left-leaning paper (the only one, by the way), for which write Croatia's top-notch journalists. Men, it goes without saying. The verb *owe* was what irked me the most. I *owe* my success, apparently, to the oft overlooked Croatian *male* essay, which deserves to be recognized and honored abroad; it would be simply unthinkable for me to owe my success to myself and my very own "voice and form." I should add that this review was almost the only public "congratulatory" gesture coming from my former domestic literary scene. That this gesture instructed me to bow down to the shadows of third-rate, and, furthermore, oft overlooked, Croatian essayists, that I admit to being the ingrate daughter of the paternal essayistic tradition—hardly warrants mention, does it? Just as there is little point in saying that the Croatian essayistic pens appear to have permanently run me out of the so-called domestic literary space. So to whom, then, am I to bow down? To my hometown "literary executioners"?[12]

---

12 Among Croatian essayists there was no mention of Miroslav Krleža, because only men can be held up in comparison to him, men who treat each other to compliments such as "upstanding pillar" (*He is an upstanding pillar of the Croatian community!*). The place of a woman in traditional space is always linked to decline (moral decline, naturally), so a woman, within these male–sexist mental constellations, is never conceptualized as an "upstanding pillar," but as "horizontal."

Misogyny in the little Balkan countries is a knee-jerk response. Misogyny is so ordinary, so deeply rooted, so ever-present, and so flagrant that no one—even those who disseminate it, even its victims—can even see it. I should also add that misogyny truly knows no geographic, class, race, gender, ethnic, or political bounds. And furthermore, misogyny often appears in camouflage, behind masks, it peeks out from places where we'd never expect to find it, from wet dreams, those innocent boyhood fantasies about the ideal, mute, partner . . .

11.

Perhaps, inspired by the episode of the two men kissing on top of the Croatian flag, we might muse on the following . . .

Apparently *flag desecration* is on the books in most countries around the world as a crime, a form of behavior subject to criminal penalty. The most common forms of *desecrating* the flag are urinating on it or burning it, though according to the United States Flag Code, "a flag, when it is in such condition that it is no longer a fitting emblem for display, should be destroyed in a dignified way, preferably by burning." In Austria, *desecration of the flag* is illegal and perpetrators may be sentenced to six months in prison. In France, *desecration of the flag* incurs a prohibitive fine or six months behind bars, in Germany someone who commits an act of *desecration* may be sentenced to as many as five years in prison, while in Croatia and Romania they may receive a sentence of up to three years. In Turkey the burning of the flag is banned and one may earn a three-year sentence by so doing, but the sentences for the actual deed of taking down the flag are far more serious. In Belgium, there is no ban for *desecration of the flag*. In

Denmark one mustn't *desecrate* the flags of other countries but one's own is fine.

Now, we wonder, what are the sentencing guidelines under Croatian law for rape, or "desecrating the honor of a woman," and how do things stand in practice? Well, it's like this. According to Croatian law "if the crime . . . resulted in the death of the raped person, or serious physical harm, or the person's health is gravely compromised, or the raped female person was thereupon impregnated, the perpetrator shall be sentenced to no less than three years in prison." Three years. According to Croatian law, the perpetrator is to be sentenced for "desecrating a woman's honor," (to use the patriarchal phrase) for just as long as one would for desecrating the Croatian flag. I have never heard of a court hearing a case about Croatian flag-burning. But I do know of many cases of the rape, beatings, and murder of Croatian women perpetrated by men. Hundreds are reported every year though many more go unreported. The victims in almost 80% of the cases know the rapist. The rapist is their husband, boyfriend, neighbor . . .

We should say, by the way, that the people of the Faroe Islands have elegantly resolved the question of their national flag by claiming that it is not possible for them to *desecrate* their flag with words or deeds. How the people of Faroe have resolved the question of women, or whether they have resolved it at all, I cannot say.

12.

Mary Beard ends her inspired article about the public voice of women with a legend. Cicero is lynched and killed. His head and right hand are on display on the speaker's platform at the Forum. Fulvia, Mark Antony's wife and a frequent victim of Cicero's speeches, arrives to inspect the head of her enemy. According to legend, Fulvia plucks a hairpin from her hair and stabs it through Cicero's tongue.

Let us stop and think now about how many symbolic hairpins would be needed to uproot the global historical practice of women's silence, and how many more it would take to ensure a global vocality and a versatility for women's voices. One voice and one hairpin don't amount to much. A powerful, massive movement is what matters for change, a multitude of strong women's and men's voices singing in unison, which will, together, obliterate the sly ways of misogyny, ways that coddle the petulant ego of many men—meanwhile assuaging the frightened hearts of many women—create billion-dollar profits in the media industry alone, delight the masses, please the politicians, and legitimize the criminality of fundamentalists of all faiths.

April 2016

La La People

Ninotchka: Must you flirt?

Leon: Well, I don't have to, but I find it natural.

Ninotchka: Suppress it!

Ninotchka, 1939

1.

For starters, let's take the freshest and most trivial example, Damien Chazelle's *La La Land* (2016). Last year and this year the film picked up all the awards it could possibly garner and earned all the millions it could earn. A thoroughly understandable mistake happened at the Oscars: because *La La Land* had won Oscars in so many other categories, no one doubted they would walk away with Best Film. So it was totally *natural* that word of their victory leaked out of the envelope and Faye Dunaway's mouth when she misread the card, a mistake rectified only a few minutes later. The Oscar for Best Film, 2017, went to *Moonlight*.

A Saturday Night Live clip, "La La Land–Interrogation," is making the rounds on YouTube. It explains in the pithiest and most eloquent fashion the quintessence of the culture we have been building for years, which we, probably, were leaning toward and within which we're flailing today as its losers or winners. A young man is brought into a police station who, without realizing he was being filmed by hidden cameras, has had the audacity to declare to his girlfriend at a restaurant his feeling that *La La Land* is not as good a movie as everybody seems to say it is. Two police officers rough up the poor skeptic and force him to say that *La La Land* is the perfect film.

2.

Ilf and Petrov are the authors of the satirical tale *How Robinson Was Created* (Как созлавался Робинсон, 1932), and those with digital savvy will be able to find a short film adaptation of the story on YouTube, directed by Eldar Ryazanov (1961). So what is it about? The editorial board of a magazine is striving to attract young readers who are tired of texts written with a "slobbering earnestness," and the editor turns to writer Moldovantsev to enliven the magazine with more adventurous material. The editor feels a new Soviet version of Robinson Crusoe would fit the bill, and the writer, whether he wants to or not, agrees. Then the editor heaps many unusual demands on the writer: after the shipwreck Robinson is not alone when he crawls out of the ocean onto the desert isle; with him are municipal government officials including the secretary, and the desert island (which, for the sake of communication, has meanwhile become a peninsula) is soon settled by shipwrecked Soviet proletarian masses. This is, after all a Soviet Robinson, is it not?

The similarity between Eldar Ryazanov's short film sketch and the Saturday Night Live video is astonishing. How is this possible? The eras have nothing to do with each other, nor do the systems and cultures, their contexts are far apart and very different. Ilf and Petrov's story was published in 1932 and filmed in 1961, while the "La La Land–Interrogation" video is a fresh parodic footnote to a film that played only a few months ago in movie theaters around the world. It behooves us to recall: the famous Kharkov congress was held in 1932 where the doctrine of socialist realism was embraced and given the official stamp of approval. The year of 1932 is usually taken as the beginning of Stalinism, which soon radically transformed not only Soviet but other communist cultures and continued on for the next twenty-odd years. This Ilf and Petrov short story (and their novels *The Golden Calf* and *The Twelve Chairs*) proved to be a powerful anticipation of what was to come. Yet how dare I link an SNL video with a satirical story by Ilf and Petrov? Have I even checked to see what century it is outside?

3.

When I was in New York I ran into an acquaintance with whom I often had passionate conversations about literature.
"What did you think about *XY*, that new book?" he asked.
And before I was able to open my mouth, he said . . .
"*It's brilliant*, don't you think?"

"Completely," I said, my heart sinking.

Why had my otherwise perceptive friend deliberately used a phrase that meant nothing, which could apply to just about anything, at any time, on any occasion? Suddenly it seemed that before me was not standing a person who had decided to respect the conventions of unwritten literary decorum, but a *homo sovieticus*, *homo duplex*, a member of the majority humanoid species which, they say, was around during the communist times, characterized by hypocrisy, a principled caution, a principled evasive lunge around conflict and paranoia, not, of course, as a diagnosis but as a lifestyle. Conflict evasion was not only defensive in nature, but it went on in the sign of a deep distrust of one's own humanoid species. Because of all that I responded in the affirmative, which only meant that any further conversation was pointless; both of us, of course, were lying and we'd go on lying.

Where does this strange, totally indefensible hypocrisy spring from, this hypocrisy surfacing in people's behavior and motivating and shaping the culture of our times, this culture which, if we were to dub it a culture of consensus, we wouldn't be far off? Does this come from fear? Will someone truly drag us down to a police station—like in the witty SNL sketch—should we admit that we're not as keen on Elena Ferrante's writing as much as others seem to be? My American acquaintance and I, each on our side of the world, each with different experiences and at different ages, are inhabiting a culture to which, whether, we like it or not, we have acquiesced. This culture is governed by money and, of course, consensus. In such a constellation, to stand up and declare in public that *La La Land* is a bad movie is tantamount to social isolation, another form of suicide. Because many who participated in the production will jump to the defense of the value of the "product," those who will be selling the product and earning money from it, those who are convinced that their investments should come back to them with a hundredfold return. The culture of consensus is a product of a powerful marketplace. Those who take part in the game will never profit from it financially. There are, however, other kinds of profit. Culture is a form of socialization. Literature, film, the visual arts, architecture, museums, opera, galleries, are realms of socialization. The digital marketplace, new digital genres (the social media) all of these are powerful springs of the global marketplace. The digital age has cut drastically into the class aspect of culture. In Communism, this was done through propaganda and communist cultural policies and praxes. Today the digital revolution has made the democratization of art possible. Culture today belongs to everyone, just as everyone, thanks to the digital revolution, has the possibility of participating in culture.

When I was flying to Zagreb, I learned from a fellow traveler that she was a math teacher from Singapore; she was traveling to Zagreb with two of her friends (Zagreb is in Croatia, isn't it?) so they could visit the *Museum of Broken Relationships*, and I realized how dangerous and difficult it would have been to tell her that the *Museum of Broken Relationships* is, perhaps, not the most exciting tourist attraction to be found in this part of Europe. Armed with their iPhones, the three young women from Singapore are children of the culture of consensus even if they have no clue that they are. And *having no clue* is, indeed, the foundation on which the culture of consensus stands.

4.

In *Ninotchka*, a classic comedy film, a young Soviet woman rejects the whole communist ideological package, not so much out of love for debonair Leon d'Algout as out of fascination with a famous cone-shaped hat. In the ideological battle between Communism and capitalism, the cone-shaped hat wins, at least as far as Ninotchka is concerned.

We have not succumbed to a mere detail of fashion, we have deliberately embraced a brand-new, powerful, profound form of hypocrisy. We are participants, creators and consumers of the modern culture of consensus. Having slipped in through the back door, the culture of consensus is quietly creeping into our lives with the firm conviction of staying here for a very long time. We live today surrounded by an orderly but also unexciting cultural environment from which the dangerous, disturbing forms of cultural life have all but disappeared: individual opinion, imagination, sincerity, intuition, polemics, subversive (genuinely subversive) artistic gestures, authenticity, stamina, rebellion, embrace of personal risk . . . According to Yevgeny Zamyatin's famous words (in a letter to Stalin), "true literature" can exist only where it is created, not by diligent and trustworthy functionaries, but by MADMEN, HERMITS, HERETICS, DREAMERS, REBELS, and SKEPTICS. Literature today (if we're speaking of literature) in the hands of the "diligent and reliable clerks," the muscle-bound jotters of countless pages, the canny negotiators and self-promoters, the authors who believe their literary efforts to be healing, only because their books sell like the holy host. Today literature is in the hands of authors whose Romanesque characters are not capable of writing a grammatically correct email or truly engage in sadomasochistic games (although they insist on both), yet they persist in foisting their tiresome lack of literacy proudly on one volume after another, in all shades of gray. Today, literature is in the hands of writers who surf as if they are freethinking, intercultural, and global, and in their novels American housewives rush off to Amsterdam to fall in love with ersatz Sufism instructors who go off and die at geographical points far more exotic than Amsterdam in their quest for spirituality. Today, literature is in the hands of writers who have dug in their heels to tell us the story of the Holocaust through the mouths of stuffed animals, monkeys and donkeys, all with the intention of shaking up our supposedly groggy imagination and to summon us to our moral responsibility . . .

5.

The mighty marketplace (which not only rules the culture of our time but *is* the culture of our time) neuters every artistic effort, doing this with everything, and so with the Russian avant-garde (and European modernism). The marketplace has neutered the culture of avant-garde resistance, commercializing it, just as it has commercialized Stalin and Stalinism. Hence the executioner and his victims find themselves out on the same market-stall counter, in the same basket, and meanwhile their differences have been lost along the way, and meanwhile ideas have been lost about art as a site of resistance, about the dynamics of art, about jettisoning the ossified forms from the *steamship of modernity*, about taking personal risk, about art *as resurrection of the word*, about art as estrangement, about art as revolution, about art that will be *a slap in the face of public taste*, which will change the world, otherwise there will be no art.

The last mass trials were a great success. There are going to be fewer but better Russians, says Ninotchka at one point. The Russians, of course, did not become better. There were just fewer of them. And then fewer still. The Russian revolutionary culture of defiance, the Russian avant-garde, was crushed by Stalinism. Literally so: they say that 1.5 million writers, artists, and thinkers were murdered in the Stalinist camps. After rehabilitation, the Russian avant-garde began its second, gradual, quiet death. This time the executioner did not have bushy whiskers. Death came in the form of the democratic, free, shiny, seductive marketplace.

6.

The entire culture of artistic subversion of the marketplace has been, with our blessing, reduced to quotes. Quotes are like household pets that compete for our attention: quotes from Joyce's *Ulysses* on a coffee mug, Duchamp's famous *Fountain* on a T-shirt. Malevich's *Sportsmen* molded in papier-mâché as souvenir dolls in various sizes, from those that can be held in the palm of the hand to garden statues. The marketplace has turned us, with our permission, into an educated mob that adores art. Art (literature, painting, film, music . . .), our favorite theme park.

And so it is that we have found ourselves on an assembly line of stripped-down, insatiable, and unstoppable production, with an expunged awareness of the continuity and purpose of our efforts. We don't know what century it is out there, nor do we hurry to name it. The age of postmodernism still defends a historical continuity, relying on strategies of homage, borrowing, parody and reconstruction, among others. Today, the only way to maintain literary-historical continuity is the act of copying, and in the process the authorship of the original is brutally ignored. So what? Are we not living at the end of history?! Who even cares at all about continuity?! The culture of the digital age evokes a chaotic mishmash of multiple, random "borrowings." The copying and rewriting are announcing the end of all art. Perhaps for that very reason, in our presentiment of the end, we declare everything brilliant: Ferrante is brilliant (to be fair, it is cause for celebration that a woman writer has finally earned the title of brilliance, because until now the self-proclaimed male defenders of the canon have had the sole right to brilliance!), Knausgaard is brilliant, and *La La Land* is brilliant . . . There is no one left who dares disagree. And if there were, would that even matter?!

We are witnesses to frequent collective, even global, hysteria. All it takes is for someone famous to dump a bucket of cold water onto their head—an ice bucket challenge—for a good cause, and a tsunami of water dumping sweeps the world; both famous and ordinary people dump buckets of cold water on their heads even though most of them have no idea why, most of them are dumping these buckets because everyone else the world over is doing it. If so, if we are all carriers of a profoundly imitative gene, if the gene responsible for our imitative skills is there in all of us, and if, moreover, it is a requisite for the existence of the human species, then we are a species vulnerable to manipulation. All it takes is for Hitler to scratch his ear, and most of us will start scratching our ears, unaware that by scratching *his* ear, Hitler was

signaling to the guards to switch on the gas chambers, and he has
received our consensus with our ear-scratching . . . If all it took
was a few years to compel most of the people of ex-Yugoslavia to
believe that they had lived differently from the way they'd actually lived, if the history they remember is not their real history,
if their good neighbor is not their good neighbor, and if they do
all this not to correct historical justice, but to help someone get
rich from it, then can we believe that the same laws do not apply
to other fields of human endeavor? How can we believe that it is
only taste ruling our literary-aesthetic criteria and not something
else? Is not the purchase of a book that millions of other readers
have bought before us the same thing as dumping a bucket of cold
water onto our heads? In both cases we have no clue why we do
it, but we are prepared to defend our choice to the death. In fact,
the less we know about what is directing our choices, the more we
are prepared to defend them. Perhaps our literary-aesthetic values
are imposed upon us, perhaps this is why *La La Land* is the most
brilliant film musical.

7.

With a New York acquaintance I went to see Julian Rosefeldt's
Manifesto, with Cate Blanchett in the lead and only role. The
unsurpassed Blanchett with her stage presence, masks, and acting
wiped away the vibrancy and potency from the manifestos she was
performing. Done in the style of the sophisticated Calvin Klein
ads in black-and-white, the movie is devoted "To all marvelous
authors of these mind-blowing manifestos." As we left the movie
theater I was proud of my friend: he didn't miss a beat, he resisted
being sucked in and it was hard not to get sucked in. Because

everyone was sucked in. His sense of being hypnotized by fear of possible social exclusion was only fleeting. We walked home slowly, chastened, afterward. There was not much to say. We had been at a brilliantly organized cultural funeral. The author of the movie forced us to pay lip service to the culture of the manifesto. I mused on the tragedy of experiencing two deaths. Many masters of the Russian avant-garde died twice: the first time when they were executed by Stalin, and the second time in our glorious artistic age—the culture of consensus.

I said goodbye to my friend and on my way to the subway station I sat for a moment on a bench in a miniature park at the intersection of West Houston and Sixth Avenue. Manhattan was awash in sunlight. An elderly woman sat down beside me, having parked a metal shopping cart next to the bench. The cart was overflowing with trash. At least that is what it initially looked like. After closer inspection I began to be able to distinguish among the things in the cart: San Pellegrino empties, Heineken cans, two empty Martinazzi bottles, and a heap of Macy's paper bags. The old lady was apparently senile, or simply feigning senility in order to avoid vexing conversations. As my eyes focused on the contents of the old woman's shopping cart, four five-pointed red stars suddenly shimmered into view within it . . .

My visual sensitivity to the five-pointed red star is understandable. In Croatia, the former Yugoslav Republic where I was born, now an independent member of the European Union, the last battle is being waged between banning the red star and fully destigmatizing the swastika. The swastika is winning the fight. With the fall of Communism and the advent of democracy, the red star was expunged from the collective Croatian field of vision, to be replaced by swastikas, black and swarming like cockroaches. This old woman on the bench beside me had forgotten, or so it seemed, why she was collecting the red stars, but her taste for the beauty of the design was intact. San Pellegrino, Martinazzi, Heineken, Macy's, and the pending celebration of the hundredth anniversary of the October Revolution . . . Ninotchka?! Could she possibly be? No, sadly, she wasn't Ninotchka, this was merely a moment of a *brilliant* deficit of artistic imagination that came over me on a bench in a New York park, in the month of May of the year 2017.

July 2017

A Fairy Tale Written by Feet

Serbs and Croats had their say
Nobody will block their way.

Primer, 1957

I should say right off the bat that I have always been indifferent to soccer. There are such people in this world, and, hey, cool it, put down your weapons, no need to shoot. We, who are indifferent to soccer, are dying out, anyway, like dinosaurs, and you, the nationally homogenized, will live on, for better or for worse. It must be because of my indifference that when the Croatian team took third place in the 1998 FIFA World Cup I experienced it as a vast explosion of national frenzy. I remember it for the words of Davor Šuker, the star of the Croatian team, when he said: "I hope Croatian writers won't be offended if we say we've written what must be the most beautiful fairy tale in the history of Croatian literature."

And here we are again, twenty years later. The Croatian landscape is studded with red-white checkerboard insignia, there's nothing like the checkerboard (*The beloved checkerboard is with me always / Wherever I go they've heard of Croats*—lyrics from a popular soccer anthem). Bombastic pop music is blaring everywhere, just as it did during the Homeland War (*Victory, combat, joy and nation / I love you so much my Croatia*), even though a quarter century has passed. Delirious with soccer madness, some Croatian citizens tumbled, in their fervor, off their balconies and crashed to their deaths, others euphorically heaved mattresses out the window, bowling over passersby on the sidewalk below, yet others bashed whatever they could bash with their cars, yet others took out loans so they could buy a ticket for a flight to Moscow where the World Cup was being held, and yet others insisted belligerently that everything that walks, swims, or flies ought to be cheering right there along with them . . . On all sides the warlike tribal drums pounded out: "Croatia, Croatia, Croatia!" From Instagram, TV screens, social media, Twitter, cell phones, and newspapers ooze news stories and scenes of nationwide festivities, pictures of the WAGs (the wives and girlfriends) of the soccer players, along with sexist comments . . . Which WAG is better looking, which has the best ass . . . Nives Celzijus, a former WAG, posted a picture to Instagram in which she poses naked, a soccer jersey draped over her hip, her bare body scribbled over in red lipstick with the names of members of the Croatian soccer team. There are other images of female fans imaginatively adorned in checkerboard designs, promising they'll take it all off if the Croats win, checkerboard children on the shoulders of checkerboard dads, checkerboard men hoarse from shouting. The tribe of Croats turn their leering faces smeared with war paint to the cameras of the world. My former compatriots look like the maddened subjects of a kingdom *through the lookingglass.* And the "queen," Croatian president Kolinda Grabar-Kitarović, decked out in red-and-white checkerboard attire, prances around in the bleachers at the Moscow stadium, racing headlong into the locker rooms to embrace the half-naked players with a maternal hug . . .

And I, nitpicker that I am, with my vision blindsided by red-and-white checkerboards, cannot help but remember that extra-extra-extra-large swastika seared into the Poljud soccer pitch and the Croatian president saying this was not the work of "local fascistoid elements," but "someone did this deliberately" to make it look as if "fascism was on the rise" in Croatia. Unobjective as I am, I cannot help but remember the "incident" at the Croatia–Israel soccer match of 2016 when the Osijek stadium chanted *Za dom spremni [For the Homeland, Prepared],* and the president said she hadn't heard the chants, and, besides, *Za dom spremni* wasn't an Ustasha slogan, but an "ancient Croatian greeting," later tainted by the Independent State of Croatia. Malicious as I am, I cannot help but remember how the Croatian president, when she visited Argentina earlier this year, gave a soccer jersey to the president of Argentina, and on that occasion said that, after World War II, many Croats "found freedom in Argentina," because they could give voice to their "love of their homeland" and "rightfully" demand "freedom for the Croatian people and their homeland." These Croats who "found freedom" in Argentina after World War II were largely Ustashas who fled after the war, including Ante Pavelić, the Independent State of Croatia's *Poglavnik* (his title as fascist leader) and Dinko Šakić, the man in charge of the Jasenovac concentration camp. Malicious as I am, I cannot forget how soccer star Davor Šuker, boasting of his "love of homeland," had his picture taken at Ante Pavelić's graveside in Madrid, and again, now, in the stands of Moscow's Luzhniki stadium—in an easygoing, friendly embrace with Croatia's President. Out of spite I settled on offering these details, among the many I could have given, which the Croatian government has been dubbing, time and time again for the last thirty years, "regrettable incidents." So many incidents have accumulated meanwhile that at this moment in Croatia any other perspective, except those well-steeped in the sweat of "love of country," is intolerable. For Croatia thrives on patriotism. Political ignoramus that I am, I cannot forget the fact that our golden boys, whether consciously or not, are camouflaging the moral, political, governmental, and economic bankruptcy of Croatia. There are elections coming up and homogenizing the people is a priority to insure that they'll vote again for their own usurpers. Croatia hasn't moved forward an inch since the end of the Homeland War, in fact it is slipping backward; tens of thousands of people are moving away in search of work; many Croats are, literally, starving, they have no jobs, nor will they be able to find them; the people in positions of authority have destroyed whatever they could destroy and devoured what there was to devour. Soccer balls slamming into goals can be counted on to distract, at least briefly, from the crimes, corruption, excesses, and incompetence of the Croatian government. The cheery red-and-white checkerboard design is a grotesque cover-up for defeat, first and foremost a defeat of morals. And the moral stumbling hasn't bypassed the soccer players themselves, they are not just spinning the soccer ball, but also vast sums of money. And besides, in countries like Croatia, soccer victories serve as a moral whitewash of the political elite who have gambled away the country's future, if it ever had one. The Croatian elite "cleansed" Croatia of some four million of their own citizens—Serbs—and have announced that the match with France will be a "storm to dwarf all storms," an oblique reference to Operation Storm when, in 1995, two hundred thousand Croatian citizens of Serbian descent were sent packing. So this "storm to dwarf all storms" declaration is a way for the elite to give the finger to Serbia while letting their own people know that soccer is a symbolic stand-in for war. This is why it is so important for our boys to win. This is why Croatian politicians will be watching the game from the stands along with the Croatian rabble, criminals, war criminals who never stood trial, state film directors, former Croatian prime ministers who are out on bail, facing charges in court, disputing massive embezzlement charges.

Meanwhile, at home, the golden Croatian boys will be greeted by hundreds of thousands of elated fans, among them Marko Perković Thompson. Thompson sings martial, patriotic, chauvinistic, Ustasha songs. With his song "Genes of Stone" [13] he touched

---

13 For those who haven't heard it, "Genes of Stone" is Thompson's wildly popular song, sung almost with the reverence of an alternative Croatian anthem. Croatian soccer players, the "fire" boys, are always inspired by it (*Genes, genes of stone, a fire burns within me*). Having *genes of stone*, aside from being *fiery*, implies a *firm hand and integrity, holy water and baptism*, in other words traditional Catholic values. The poem mentions 1945 (*'45 was a bad year, we scattered worldwide*), referring to the fall of Pavelić's Nazi state and the flight of Ustashas from the country (with Argentina as the most popular destination). However, as Thompson suggests, there are reasons for optimism, because *the swallows have returned, new grape vines are growing, new children are being born*, who are, surprise, surprise, of *blue blood, with white faces*. This last verse of Thompson's is a creative racist addendum to Franjo Tuđman's famous words about his wife not being "a Serb or a Jew." Tuđman introduced to his vision of the modern state the concept of knighthood ("valiant Croatian knights"), thereby effectively feudalizing the country, by giving his symbolic "knights" more than a real fief. Thompson's poetic and visual requisitory bristles with chivalric symbolism. Nobody has ever remarked that the knights seem to be the homosexual fantasy of the

the hearts of many hundreds of fervid fans. A day or two later, Zlatko Dalić, the manager of the Croatian team and the person most deserving of the silver medal the Croatian soccer team won, went to the town of Varaždin to celebrate their World Cup success with the community there, and, again, there on the stage was Marko Perković Thompson, and, with him, surprise, surprise, Velimir Bujanec, the most prominent media spokesperson for the boom of the Croatian neo-Ustasha movement. And only a few days later the Croatian Historical Museum opened an exhibit of photographs, *Indescribable!!*, taken during the spectacular welcome parade when the Croatian soccer team returned to Zagreb. And on social media, on the portals and in the papers, a list began circulating again of "enemies of Croatia." The victory of the Croatian soccer team felt like a wartime victory, and so anyone who didn't voice enthusiasm for the victory was pigeonholed as a political enemy of Croatia.

In closing, who am I that I dare rain on the triumphalist parade of almost four million Croats! An ordinary author. A Croatian author? No, not at all, it would be immodest of me to foist myself on a literature whose most beautiful fairy tales were written by feet. For such a thing I am missing the attributes: the feet of a soccer player and *genes of stone.*

July 2018

Croatian defenders, nationalists, and neofascists. Maybe this is why the Croats find breaking things off with their enemy Serbs so difficult, just as the Serbs can't bear to disengage from their enemy Croats, Bosnians, and Albanians.

There's Nothing Here!

They lowered him down. Partway he went, but was afraid of being lowered into the abyss. He tugged on the rope and they brought him up. Once they'd pulled him out, they asked, "What did you see?"

"No bottom," he replied.

Roma fairy tale

1.

The culture of bathing has played a pivotal role in the history of civilization. Although it, the history of civilization, is rooted in wars, conquests, famous battles, and male heroics, there were those, like the old Romans, who left behind them something useful as well. Wherever they passed, Romans built public baths, Roman hot springs, and references to the goddess Minerva, whose name adorns many a hot-springs hotel. Turks, Arabs, the Islamic world, have given civilization public baths, *hammams*, and made affordable to all the habit of bathing. Northern Europe has saunas or *banyas* or baths, the folk mythology of water, legends about miraculous cures and rejuvenation, mythical beings, river

179

fairies, a whole water-bound imaginary. The Russian *banya* is an inseparable part of Russian everyday life, but also a frequent motif in legends, fairy tales, and literature (Mayakovsky, Zoshchenko), and in movies as well. The plot of Eldar Ryazanov's movie *The Irony of Fate or Enjoy Your Bath!* (1975), begins in a Russian bathhouse; in David Cronenberg's *Eastern Promises* (2007) a London *banya* frequented by the Russian underworld serves as the site for brutal showdowns. Famous western European spa cities, such as Baden-Baden, were visited by Tolstoy and Dostoevsky, while Karlovy Vary was a favorite haunt for Beethoven, Liszt, Chopin, Peter the Great, Turgenev, and, again, Tolstoy. Milan Kundera wasn't wrong when he set the plot of *The Farewell Party*—his little pearl of a novel—in a Czech spa.

One way or another I keep stumbling over hot springs, even when my travels take me there for non-hot-springs reasons, such as when I was invited to the University of Warwick. While there, I explored the Royal Leamington Spa, active in the nineteenth century and visited twice by Queen Victoria herself. I visit hot springs for more reasons than just my bad back. While there I limber up my perceptive capabilities. Hot springs have a sobering and entrancing effect on me, not only do they confront me with my medical needs but also with my social status, meanwhile fostering a feeling of general well-being, giving wings to the illusion that things are far better than they actually are.

Abi Wright, an expert on the fast-expanding spa industry, claims that the price of a day at the spa runs from £20 to £2000. The clientele select their place in the social hierarchy. And right here, in this zone, the dynamic is the most intense. People (shall we call them *hotspringers?*) travel for many miles, as do the Croatian retirees who in semi-secrecy sneak off by bus to the Vrućica baths in the Serbian part of Bosnia and Herzegovina—Republika Srpska. The retiree-traitors pay the "despised" Serbs for spa services because the Bosnian Serb spas are cheaper and better in quality than the spas in Croatia. Spas are, therefore, a test of patriotism. When it comes to spas, patriotism gives way to frugality. There you have a detail which makes sense only to Croats and Serbs. The keys for entering one's password on ATMs in the Republika Srpska offer two language options: English or *local*. This, too, is something only *local* people understand. The language of the *locals* is dragon-tongue: it flicks its three equal tongues, Serbian, Croatian, and Bosnian. And the entire modern complex of hot springs, known as Banja Vrućica, is dominated by an Orthodox shrine, one in a series of recently built, standard-form Orthodox, Muslim, and Catholic places of worship scattered across the landscape of Bosnia and Herzegovina, reminiscent of standard-form Chinese restaurants.

2.

Why do I find myself drawn to hot springs? I enjoy playing the anthropologist on a clandestine mission: I watch the subtle flow of people and money where one least expects or notices it. The spas I have in mind were built on earlier Austro-Hungarian foundations (and these were raised on Roman spas), or they sprouted during the Socialist era. Most have not been recently renovated, or if they have, the renovation has been patchy. Many are now in ruins. They were occupied by war veterans from the most recent war (1991–1995) who—beset by alcohol, drugs, and troubles—vented their anger on the hot springs. Under the roofs of spas, the old communist utopia (the dream of highly professional, well-lit, and modern sanatoriums for all) stagnates and mingles with a dose of postcommunist human despair, along with mildew festering on the tiles, and the yellowed hydromassage baths. I read the things around me differently than does the spa staff, postcommunist kids, those cute humanoids whose memory cards have been erased. I'm older than they are and, though I may have no proof, I know a second level lies beneath the surface, and beneath the second there's a third . . .

In the time of Yugoslavia, rivers of Slovenes, Croats, Bosnians, Serbs, and Macedonians with aching bones streamed to a sanatorium known as the Dr. Simo Milošević Institute in the Montenegrin coastal town of Igalo. Everything was paid for with wanton abandon (or so they say today) by the Yugoslav health insurance system. The institute is an imposing edifice of Yugoslav socialist architecture with probably the largest hotel lobby in the region, and a certain number of capacious hotel rooms, but the place is equipped with a disproportionately small swimming pool. Nowadays, the building excites both admiration and pity, as do all examples of neglect, especially the neglect that followed the fall of Communism and the advent of the misconstrued democracy. The vestiges of the communist era, along with the Adriatic Sea and its affordability, attract the elderly Norwegians, Danes, and Dutch, while the sanatorium staff has been holding their breath in hopes, for years, that the facility would be purchased by a wealthy Norwegian and transformed into a high-priced, classy wellness center. The character of Dr. Škréta, a spa gynecologist, (in Kundera's *The Farewell Party*), who dreams of being adopted by Bertlef, a filthy rich American, is in fact a precise anticipatory metaphor for today's postcommunist Europe. Postcommunist Europe sees itself as a swanky wellness center frequented by an assortment of rich men who have nothing better to do than satisfy the fantasies of the locals and adopt them once and for all.

Igalo is a destination not merely for Scandinavians with aching bones, but also for the poorer class of Russians. The crassly wealthy Russians have been buying up land on the Montenegrin mountainsides where they build lavish mansions with bird's-eye views of the sea. The poorer Russians meanwhile buy modest apartments in unsightly socialist high-rises. I met a Russian woman, an elderly lady, and her son. They'd purchased one of those little apartments and spend every summer in Igalo.

After the Russians bought the Karlovy Vary spa in the Czech Republic and conquered with cash what they'd failed to conquer earlier with tanks, after they turned Montenegro into their resort and the proud Montenegrins into their waitstaff, money launderers, bodyguards, and the like—they moved on in a northwesterly direction and occupied Rogaška Slatina, a Slovenian spa. The Yugoslavs were, long ago, united by brotherhood and unity; now, or so it seems, they are united by the Russians. In vain did Tito declare his historical "no" to Stalin. Today, post-Yugoslavs are saying a willing "yes" to investments from Putin's circle.

How do I know? In September 2016, I stayed for five days at the Rogaška Grand Hotel, which had been purchased by a wealthy Russian. It should be said that the new owner invested not a cent in renovations. The only novelty were the Russian channels on the

TV sets in the guest rooms. Over my five days there I watched my fill of Russian TV and learned that the visible, superficial glow of the "western" style of life is easy to imitate. After Perestroika and the fall of the wall, even the most backward Russian "country hick," such as Vladimir Zhirinovsky, learned that one must redesign oneself, have a good dentist, hairdresser, plastic surgeon, optician, brand-name attire, and a personal trainer, and package up one's personal Perestroika. This is something all the offspring of postcommunists know. The Croatian president, Kolinda Grabar Kitarović, knows it. Her sudden surge in political popularity can be attributed to the fact that she successfully shed excess pounds, and that, as far as fashion is concerned, she closely follows Carrie Bradshaw in *Sex and the City*. While watching Russian TV, I discovered that the hard-core, censored, Soviet Communist television program was incomparably better in quality than today's "uncensored" variety. Today, as from everywhere else, raw uncensored stupidity seeps from Russian TV channels.

Russian guests enjoy strolling around swathed in white terry cloth robes while obediently sipping the vapid mineral water. At the neighboring hotel, the Donat (named for the mineral water bottled there), the visitors are each given their own water mug with their personal number, and then, mug in hand, they enter the glassed-in temple dedicated to the mineral water goddess, Donat Mg, known fondly as Lady Donat. The Russians enjoy this collective religious rite through which they pay homage to the anti-obstipational mineral, Magnesium the Great. One's personal mug with its special number costs seven euros a day; outside the "temple" there are places where the same water can be had for free. In front of the Donat stands a monument to Slovenian

Communist Boris Kidrič, organizer of the Slovenian anti-fascist resistance during the German occupation. Kidrič is hip-deep in the marble pedestal, as if he's sinking in quicksand. One of his arms is lowered, the other raised, exactly as if he were holding a mug of Lady Donat and toasting someone. His hand, however, is holding nothing; hotel guests often tuck a posy of wildflowers into this hand, the one clasping the nonexistent mug. The Boris Kidrič statue serves as proof that the farsighted Slovenes are not as destructive toward their anti-fascist monuments as are the fervid Croats, especially if the dead anti-fascists can serve as a mug holder or a vase or stir nostalgic sentiments in potential real-estate clients or solvent guests.

3.

In April 2016, a few months before my stay in Rogaška Slatina, I'd spent two weeks at the Daruvar hot springs (formerly Roman!), which lie some sixty miles to the east of Zagreb. I went, resolved to do something for my spine, which was worn down after many years of desk-sitting. Even writing has its occupational hazards—though bone and muscle aches are not the only, nor the most dangerous, ones of my occupation.

Small provincial towns like Daruvarske Toplice, with little to offer but thermal waters and a minority Czech community, have an inspirational effect on me; when I'm short of things to keep me busy, they provide ferment for my artistic imagination. While I'm exercising in the heated pool, for instance, surrounded by "ossified" patients like me, I amuse myself by picturing an opera. I imagine the parts sung by the physical therapist, the hotel receptionist, the cooks at the hot springs restaurant, the waiters, the hotel guests, the retirees, young athletes, nurses, massage therapists, and patients.

In the pool, where every fifteen minutes powerful gushes of water spurt from the jets, I eavesdrop on the conversations of the elderly males, who have arranged themselves strategically around the jets so that nobody else can come close. They talk about the making of smoked sausages, the advantages of one kind of food over another (*There's no poultry like pork; Who gives a shit about swiss chard and potatoes, vegetables aren't for us Slavonians*), about politics and the freedom that dawned twenty-five years before *with the collapse of stinking old Yugoslavia*, about the Yugoslav *dungeon of the peoples*, the glorious Croatian victory over the Serbs, who, by the way, *should all have been done away with back in the '90s*. The males thump each other on the back with their words, approving (*Oh, yes, yes! So right! Like I've always said!*), parading their own importance, especially in the struggle against the Serbs, making a point of their own political savvy and insight (*damn straight, I saw this coming!*)

Here—a discreet wink to my potential literary interpreters; the hot springs are a literary device, a source of defamiliarization: the shift of the ordinary into an out-of-ordinary environment where heroes, their actions, and words, acquire a new, "dislocated" significance, a different hue and tone. And while we're on the subject of hot springs, literary devices, and the Czech minority living in the Daruvar area, the Czech writer Bohumil Hrabal was a master of defamiliarization. His greatness lies in his sincere love of humanity, the human males and the females, the losers and the winners, the stupid and the smart, the fortunate and the deadbeats. Hrabal was like a sort of literary Jesus Christ—if we can imagine Jesus Christ to be a serious beer drinker—who loved all humankind with the same love, understood them all, and forgave them. I envy Hrabal his unique alchemical talent for turning garbage into gems, and his love of mankind that sparkles from his books like an inexhaustible water fountain. If Hrabal were here now, he'd have a beer with these men; he'd chat with them about his weak bladder and taking a piss with the same high-flying enthusiasm as about the stars; he'd enjoy floating in the warm swimming pool, harkening to the layers of sound: the endearing chirp of the birds on the one hand and the doltish honk of the people on the other. All people are God's creatures and deserving of love, and this love is what carries the diminutive waiter Dítě, hero of the novel *I Served the King of England*, through the prewar period, Fascism, and the postwar Czech communist period with the same ease. The political systems, wars, ideologies, losses, and gains—all these toy with the fate of Hrabal's protagonist, but he survives, ever indestructible, preserving his love for life.

I lack Hrabal's compassion for human stupidity (is there a form of stupidity other than human?). Instead of soaking in the warm water of empathy, I tend to fly into righteous indignation, as if "avenging angel" were part of my job description, though because of my aching back I'm in no shape to wield a righteous sword. What am I, therefore, left with? To "iron" my crooked spine and grumble to the point of exhaustion. True, the Daruvar spa is hardly Mann's *Der Zauberberg* and I'm no Thomas Mann. Nor am I Bohumil Hrabal. Consequently, I don't deserve the divine Czech spas.

At the Daruvar spa, where there was nothing more interesting than the TV set in my room with its three channels, I came across Mladen Kovačević's documentary *Unplugged* (2013). The unusual documentary portrays two people somewhere in southern Serbia, a peasant and a retiree, she, having worked abroad as a guest worker. The two of them are perhaps the last remaining masters of the skill of playing music on leaves. *Earlier everybody knew this, nobody was mute, now we're all mute!* says the peasant, a crank and freethinker. *Even the birds no longer sing, they're all demoralized!* While she selects which leaves are best suited for playing, the retired guest worker declares, with confidence: *I can even play a nettle leaf!*

This assertion by the self-taught artist—*I can even play a nettle leaf!*—chilled me and slithered like a snake it into my nightmares. Ever since then I sometimes dream that I bring a nettle leaf to my lips and try to make a sound, any sound, but I can't, I don't know how, I don't have what it takes. My lips sting, they feel as if they're bleeding, I touch them, they're swollen, on my fingertips there are spots of blood . . . *Occupational hazards*, I think in my dream. Serves me right, I think. My lips swell up but I keep puffing away, as if hypnotized. I look around for other leaves to serve as a balm, but there aren't any. The nettle, the one in my dream, is what I've been given, me in particular.

4.

Topusko is some fifty miles southeast of Zagreb, almost at the border with Bosnia. In May 2018, I spent a full two weeks there and didn't see a single Russian. But through the Top-Terme Hotel barreled a group of Chinese, a Korean group tiptoed in and out, and Croatian elementary school students galloped through. Several Croatian police officers were also sniffing around, which I wouldn't have known if I hadn't happened to ride up in the elevator with one of them, and the elevator, being an elevator, didn't get stuck, exactly, but did stop for a few minutes between floors. There was also a group of tall, robust young men, Dutch, staying at the hotel, who stood out dramatically against the backdrop of the elderly, semi-invalid, local guests. The Chinese guests, who, with their suitcases, elbowed their way energetically into the elevator, I saw only once, briefly, and the Dutch appeared only once for breakfast. The Chinese and Koreans were not products of my overactive imagination but part of the routine tourist crowd. The hotel was on the route for tour groups headed for the Plitvice Lakes National Park, only ten to fifteen miles away, and tourist agencies used it for affordable accommodation.

In the evening I watched the Korean group around the pool. There was a full moon. The Koreans stood in a circle, clapping and singing. I don't know why but I felt sure they were singing a song about a rabbit on the moon; wherever the Chinese, Koreans, and other Asian visitors go, the moon goes with them. And the moon is steered, boat-like, by a rabbit . . .

5.

At a little tourist office on the main street (there didn't seem to be any others) I ask the man at the counter a few questions.

"Do you have any information about Topusko, a brochure for tourists, anything?"

"We've got nothing . . ." he says, putting emphasis on the word *nothing*.

"Nothing?"

"Nothing's what we've got."

The emphasis on the word *nothing* is still there.

"What can you give me then?"

"I can print you out the schedule of the times buses leave for Zagreb . . ."

"Okay, thanks, if you would."

As he hands me the bus schedule he's printed, he adds, "I can give you the phone number of a local taxi service."

"Sure . . ."

I take the business card with the name of the taxi service on it: "Drive, Miško!" I clutch the card as if it is the straw that will save me from drowning, touched by the reference to the *Sijan* movie. There are some things that haven't been completely forgotten, I think.

"I was wondering if I might ask you something. There used to be a Partisan hospital up there in the Petrova hills. I know we came here once with my school class on an field trip."

"Gone."

"Gone?"

"All those things have gone to ruin, overgrown with weeds, there's nothing left," he says, again with emphasis on the *nothing*.

"But wasn't there a famous meeting held here of the State Anti-Fascist Council for the National Liberation of Croatia?"

"Maybe," he says, cautiously.

"Well, where was the meeting held?"

"Gone."

"How could it be gone! Isn't there a building?"

"Gone. Torn down."

"Fine, but if you know it's been torn down, then you must know where it stood."

"By the hotel. There's a plaque that explains everything."

So I leave the utterly empty office, where, at the counter, as if at the front desk of a nonexistent hotel, sits the man. Over the entrance are the words *Tourist Office*, clear as day. Several of the houses along the main street are in ruins and there are trees and grass growing up through them, reminiscent of documentaries about Chernobyl. I carefully tuck the piece of paper with the bus schedule into my purse. On my way back to the hotel I wonder whether perhaps the office where I just was would be gone by the next day, leaving *nothing*.

Several hours earlier, I'd been talking with the doctor. He was over eighty, he'd retired years before, and came here by bus from Zagreb, though only on Mondays. There was no in-house doctor, four of them had already left, going wherever anyone would hire them. Here he was more feigning his profession than actually performing it, a placeholder, no more, no less.

A few days later in the waiting room for therapy I stopped a girl in a white lab coat.

"Excuse me, there's no light in the women's bathroom."

"Huh."

"Exactly why I'm telling you. The bulb needs changing . . ."

"I know *nothing* about that . . ."

"Don't you work here?"

"I'm, like, just an intern."

6.

At breakfast I asked the muscular young men, the Dutch, what they're doing in this place where there is *nothing*. They answered my questions reluctantly, maybe because I admitted I hadn't noticed their vehicles in the parking lot. Everybody else knew who they were and why they were here as soon as they saw their vehicles. The massage therapist explained: the boys were off-roaders. The local people called them the "mud pack" because they loved being up to their ears in mud. Somewhere nearby, a Cro-Trophy competition was on. There was a Russian, a maniac, who came every year with his armored car . . .

"Armored car?"

"A tank, really. Straight out of Mad Max!" explained the masseuse.

I heard the other side of the story from Boba, the woman who drove the taxi. Such total devastation of the environment was permitted in Croatia, but not in other EU countries. This is why the "mud pack" was so crazy about Croatia. On our way into the Petrova hills, Boba showed me a whole hillside that had been gutted, savaged, and stripped bare. "This is what it looks like after the boys leave," said Boba. She knew this whole region like the inside of her pocket, she'd been volunteering as a firefighter for years. Setting the woods on fire was a popular local sport. Boba knew all the villages and hamlets, she was born here, she delivered what the elderly people in the abandoned villages needed: food, medicine, supplies, fuel, lamps, candles, where there was no electric power; in most of those places there was *nothing* left . . . I couldn't tear my eyes away, *raped forests*, I said, and then felt shame, the words came nowhere near to describing what I was seeing.

7.

I reserved a taxi on the bright and sunny May day I met Boba, a willowy middle-aged blonde. She apologized straight away, her husband, she said, was busy. She hoped I didn't mind having her drive me instead of Miško. Indeed, I didn't mind at all. I was interested in having a look at a famous war monument by Vojin Bakić in the Petrova hills. Bakić was a sculptor and a Croatian Serb. Why even mention his ethnicity? Because his ethnicity set the parameters for his life, his fate as an artist, his place in the world. And even if his ethnicity was a detail he may have cared little about, it became a noose around his neck. In Croatian Wikipedia, Bakić is described as a "Croatian sculptor of Serbian descent." Bakić's four brothers were killed by the Ustashas during World War II. He completed his most spectacular work, *A Monument to the Uprising of the People of Kordun and Banija*, in 1981 and died eleven years later. During the 1991–1995 war, there was a systematic effort undertaken to destroy his monuments, six of which were destroyed completely, while four were supposedly only "partially damaged." Bakić was born in Bjelovar, where he left several monuments. His *Man from Bjelovar* sculpture, commemorating the tragic fate of his family, was blasted to pieces in 1991; after being repaired and restored, it was remounted in 2010. His

Man from Gudovac statue (Gudovac being a village near Bjelovar) was blown up and the fragments melted down. A stainless-steel monument in the village of Kamenska was blown up in 1992 and the shards used to manufacture dishes. A monument to the Partisans in the village of Bačkovica was blown up and melted down, and a statue to the fallen fighters in Čazma was also destroyed. Six of Bakić's abstract sculptures in crystal, installed at Dotrščina[14] Monument Park, were stolen and destroyed. Of the three busts (all by Vojin Bakić)—portraying linguist Ljudevit Jonke, and the poets S. S. Kranjčević and I. G. Kovačić—that stood out in front of the Karlovac public library, the bust of Ivan Goran Kovačić—author of the chilling poem "The Pit," inspired by events from World War II—was destroyed (2004). Unknown vandals stole the commemorative plaque mounted on the Bakić house in Bjelovar and smashed the inscription on the family tomb at the Bjelovar cemetery. The city government has renamed the street that once bore the names of the Bakić brothers.

During Operation Storm, which began on August 5, 1995, the Croatian army torched villages, and killed several hundred innocent civilians, including the elderly and children. The World War II monument, *The Uprising of the People of Kordun and Banija*, standing at the highest point in the Petrova Gora hill range, has been abandoned since 1995 to wayward vandalism, and has been

---

14 The Dotrščina Monument Park was designed to honor and commemorate the victims of Fascism. The Ustashas brought Croatian anti-fascists there, murdered them, and then buried them in mass graves, including 2000 Communists. According to official data from 1985, approximately 700 anti-Fascists were put to death there. In 1990, after the change of government, the building of monuments in the park was halted and ever since then Dotrščina has been ravaged. To be fair, I should add that there are young artists and activists who are working as volunteers, with no institutional affiliation, trying to preserve this unique memorial park by the skin of their teeth.

"partially" destroyed. For a full twenty-three years the local and state authorities have turned a blind eye to protecting the monument and preventing its further devastation.

The spectacle of Bakić's masterpiece in ruins gave me a sudden panic attack. I felt I'd never in my whole life seen a more appalling sight. The monument resembled an immense whale carcass: the gnawed protruding bones, the rot, the disgorged internal organs, everything removable had been stripped away. On the roof terrace of the monument, initially designed as a vantage point from which to enjoy the magnificent view, somebody had mounted an antenna, rising skyward like a cynically brandished middle finger. Boba didn't know whose antenna it was or what purpose it served. On one of the stripped-bare concrete walls I noticed a little sticker with a photograph of Emma Goldman and the quote: "The most violent element in society is ignorance." The time was noon, and around us spread a graveyard hush. I felt as if the saplings, weeds, and grass that were pushing their way up through the cracks in the concrete were holding their breath and saving their strength to stave off the monument's plunge into nothingness. I felt—as in the popular Partisan song "On Konjuh Mountain"[15]—that the leaves truly were singing "sorrowful songs," and that "pine and fir, maple and birch" had bowed in a genuflection of respect. The woods, over which a ruddy shadow briefly passed ("The red woods came out in leaf"), were not red, as in the song, from the "blood of the Husino miners," but, this time, from shame. I was shaken by an eerie presentiment, my heart sank for a moment at

---

15 *Konjuh planinom* [On Konjuh Mountain], a Partisan song, written in 1941, verses by Miloš Popović-Đurin, music by legendary Yugoslav composer Oskar Danon.

the prospect of *something* to come, although beyond that *something* stood *nothing*, no image, no thought, no sense. The *something* was invisible, shapeless, no smell or taste, like radiation. A warning sprayed onto the concrete wall, "Beware: standing near the monument is dangerous" suddenly seemed apt.

Boba and I got into the car and made our way back. And just as each of us was lost in thought on the road to Topusko, my phone rang.

"Auntie, are you in your room?"

"No, hon, why?"

"Quick, go to your room and turn on the TV!"

"Why?"

"Do you really not know? Today's the most important day of the decade! Harry and Meghan's wedding!" reported my fifteen-year-old niece, breathless. I thought how quickly she'd embraced the phrase served up to her by the media: *the most important day of the decade* . . .

I thought of how there are so many parallel realities, even among those closest to me, such as my reality here and the reality my niece inhabits. Who in the world cares about a monument that's been destroyed, no matter how breathtaking it may have been as a work of art, and who am I to take this on and call out others for failing to maintain it? I myself am no longer capable of saying how and why this all happened, though I have been tearing out my hair over it for a quarter century now. And, furthermore, isn't this wordlessness, this inability to transmit experience, the burden of the future?

8.

The fate of Vojin Bakić's sculptures is more the rule than the exception. The landscape of postcommunist countries is strewn with these ruins. Everywhere there are concrete eyesores half overgrown with grass and weeds, monuments of "slumbering concrete."[16] There are industrial ruins, ruins of statues, devastated residential areas, failed projects, abandoned projects, closed schools, torched houses, destroyed farms, ripped-out electrical lines, torn-out windows, neglect, abandonment . . . There are small ruins, big ruins, mega ruins, such as the motel that lies along the highway between Niš and Belgrade with what must be the largest truck-parking lot in this part of Europe, outfitted with public shower stalls the size of a studio apartment, cavernous restaurant halls, shops, and all sorts of other things . . . The motel was built at a time when southern Serbia was thought to be the main artery between Western Europe and the south: Bulgaria, Greece, Turkey. But then came the war, and all through traffic ceased, time stopped, people drifted off to sleep, they went to war and are still at it, as if trapped inside Márquez's *A Hundred Years of Solitude*.

"Slumbering concrete," wrongly ascribed only to the collapse of Communism and its architectural aesthetic, attracts the attention today of freaks and nostalgia hunters, lovers of "communist" chic

---

16 *Betonski spavači* [Slumbering Concrete] is a four-part documentary by director Saša Ban (begun in 2016) about the many examples of Yugoslav modernist architecture (barely fifty years old) that have, since the dissolution of Yugoslavia, been abandoned to ruin, devastation, and collapse.

and concrete decadence: the historians, snobs, documentarians, cultural trendsetters, architects, and archeologists of Socialist modernism. But few are thinking about the new owners, the "winners," who without a trace of mercy are jettisoning and burning the old "furniture" and moving in their own. Skopje is a city of winners with "artistic" pretensions, a city which has, of late, installed more public sculptures than it has inhabitants, it is a Balkan Disneyland. Fountains, triumphal arches, horses with indecently bulging rumps and disproportionately gigantic hooves, famous horsemen: Alexander the Great, Philip II of Macedon, the historical mothers of historical personalities with aggressively bulbous breasts. The Vardar—which can hardly be called a river anymore, especially not the river where, in the words of a lyrical Macedonian folk song, "Biljana washed her linens white"—now with all the new bridges spanning it, three vast concrete ships sunken into the riverbed and three vast concrete vases built into the river floor. All this new, massive, triumphalist "furniture" has visually "eaten" Skopje alive and the few exemplars of modernist architecture (by architect Kenzō Tange) built after the major earthquake of 1963.

Let us, for a moment, imagine pink plastic flamingoes, garden gnomes in all sizes, sunset-motif wallpaper, and all the people who own these flamingoes, gnomes, wallpaper, embarking on a crusade against everything we have always thought of as "culture," jettisoning all the "furniture" from MoMA, the Guggenheim, the Louvre, the British Museum, and the other temples of the art of "our civilization," and moving themselves into the emptied space with the blessings of the powers that be. Even sci-fi movies don't go that far, yet this is precisely what has been happening in real life, though in a small place where few people take such things seriously. The illiterate (it is they, for God's sake, who are everywhere ascendant!) are visiting their terror upon the literate (haven't the literate always been a minority, anyway?).

Croatian war veterans are protesting out in front of theaters, seeking a ban on any play that denigrates their role in the defense of the country. Hysterical pro-life organizations are demanding that contemporary literary works be stricken from the curriculum if the titles they abhor are promoting sex, or homosexuality, or whatever else they perceive as perversions. Certain members of the Croatian Parliament have been making public declarations against certain women writers, demanding that their books be struck from Croatian literature, although they haven't, themselves, read the books, and couldn't anyway, as they are illiterate. The fact that they're illiterate doesn't prevent them, however, from rancorously imposing their opinions about everything, including literature. Politicians, criminals, murderers, thieves, and the nouveaux riches take their seats at every theater and cinematic premiere, at every opening of a show, and share their opinions about it with an air of knowing authority. The Croatian defenders have recently succeeded in preventing a concert by a Belgrade pop singer, scheduled to be held in Karlovac. The Association of Widows of the Croatian Defenders of the Homeland War sabotaged a festival to be held in Petrinja of a special ancient form of folk chanting using the syllable "oy" known as *ojkanje*, claiming that *ojkanje* is not a tradition local to Petrinja. Why were the widows of Croatian defenders so fixated on good old *ojkanje*? Because they felt this was a Serbian form of chant, and that was enough to insult the memory of their late husbands, who gave their lives to defend their homeland from Serbian *ojkanje*. The reasoning put forth by the widows goes hand in hand with a sentiment voiced by Franjo Tuđman when he announced the dawn of freedom in a speech in the town of Sinj in 1990. This was to be a new age in which *the Croatian people would be free to sing their songs, their innocent songs*. The Croats chant their *gangas* and *reras*, and the Serbs chant their *ojkanje*. Period.

9.

"We'll be going out with Gramps for a bit of a stroll . . ." says a woman in response to my question of what she'll be up to after dinner.

The couple has been at my table since my first day at the spa; we were assigned to sit together during meals. On the table stands a menu for lunch and supper, offering a selection of three dishes.

"We ordered pork schnitzels with mashed potatoes for our lunch tomorrow, didn't we, Gramps?" says the woman.

"We"—she and her husband—are retirees. He is taciturn, bumbly when he walks and talks. As if aware of this, he tends to keep quiet. She calls him *Gramps* and treats him like a plush teddy bear, a toy fate handed her when she was a girl, and without which, ever since, she has never gone anywhere. The toy seemingly has no opinion. "My *Gramps* is a little out of it, aren't you, *Gramps?*"

She, of course, immediately *nosed* out that I'm a writer. To be fair it wasn't she but her daughter, who lives in America. When she told her daughter whom she'd been sitting with, her daughter immediately asked around and figured out who I was. The daughter adores my books. Do give my regards to the writer, she said . . .

I know the woman who is sitting across from me like the inside of my pocket. Hypocrisy is inscribed in her genetic code, this is how her parents raised her, this is her environment: express your opinion, but take care not to offend. They worked honestly their whole lives, she and her husband, but life didn't pamper them, it dealt them blows left and right. I spot a gleam in the woman's eyes. She watches me with cunning from behind her spectacles. She sees through me, as soon as I take my seat at their table. Arrogance and servility are her fuel, arrogance and servility course through her veins, yes, the weapons of the weak, perhaps, but people like them survive . . .

"We haven't heard a word about that, have we, *Gramps*?"

"It's true, they are right here across the border, in Velika Kladuša, thousands of refugees from Syria, Afghanistan, Iran . . ."

"Oh come on, we've never had refugees, what would they do here?" she says as if we're discussing Asian tiger mosquitoes, not people.

"Oh, it's true. The hotel is full of police. Haven't you noticed? They go out from here and collar refugees, and when they collar them, they send them back over the border, to Bosnia."

"We didn't know. I don't watch anything on TV, do I, *Gramps*, the news or the soap operas. I'm terribly out of touch."

"You're best off treating the news as if it's a soap opera, and the soap operas as if they're news. Only then will everything start making sense," I say.

She stops, squints through her glasses, sniffs danger like a rabbit. She senses I'm joking but she doesn't get it, and if she doesn't get it, that means I'm snubbing her. And she will not allow herself to be snubbed by some writer or other nobody except her kooky daughter has ever heard of . . .

"We're off, we are, for a little stroll, *Gramps* and I," says the woman and the couple rises from the table.

10.

On the bus back to Zagreb, I passed through the region that used to be called Krajina. I hadn't known, as I wasn't paying attention, that it was mostly Serbs who lived there. During World War II many Serbs were killed here by the Ustashas, and Serbs fled into the woods and joined Tito's Partisans. Lika, Banija, Kordun—all these were Partisan strongholds. While the bus drove through Glina, over and over again my eyes, through the bus window, spotted the names of Ban Josip Jelačić, Franjo Tuđman, and Josip Runjanin (a composer, and author of the Croatian national anthem *Lijepa naša domovina* [Oh Beautiful, Our Homeland]) on one street sign after another, perhaps because the signs were the only new accent to be seen on the otherwise ramshackle old houses. Aside from the fact that the town seemed deserted, there was a notable shortage of Croatian names deemed suitable for the naming of the streets, parks, and squares. Perhaps for this very reason, another name jumped out at me along with Tuđman's, Jelačić's, and Runjanin's: one street was actually called Croatian Street, yes: *Hrvatska ulica*, indeed.

In 1941, the Ustashas slaughtered innocent civilians of Serbian ethnicity in the Glina Orthodox church. The church was torn down after the mass murder, and ten years later the Communist authorities built a commemorative ossuary there. Later still, on that same spot, a memorial center was built to commemorate the victims of Fascism. The number of Ustasha massacre victims ranges, according to various sources, from two hundred to over two thousand people. Croatian Wikipedia suggests that perhaps the massacre never even happened. After Operation Storm, the taking of Glina, and the expelling of civilians of Serbian ethnicity from the region, the Croatian authorities renamed the memorial center the Croatian Center. And more recently, a memorial plaque was installed in Glina, which honors the murdered and imprisoned soldiers of the Armed Forces of the Independent State of Croatia and the German Wehrmacht.

11.

Glina swam back into view some two months later, on August 5, 2018, on the Day of Victory and Homeland Thanksgiving and the Day of the Croatian Defenders. Croatian president Kolinda Grabar-Kitarović chose that day to honor Croatian generals Ante Gotovina and Ivan Čermak with the highest medals awarded by Croatia, which they earned for their shining role in Operation Storm. That same day, Marko Perković Thompson—icon of the numerically superior Croatian right wing—held a spectacular concert in Glina, which, according to media estimates, was attended by about one hundred thousand people. Judging by the videos that have been circulating on the internet, many of the young concert goers were dressed in black T-shirts, black pants, black boots, black berets, and flashy body tattoos. The Croatian Defense Forces, known by its acronym, HOS, are a militaristic-clerical group (*brothers and sisters*) and a political party that in its iconography proudly displays the fascist greeting *Za dom spremni*. Some of the young girls looked like an Ustasha version of Lolita in braids and black berets, wearing body-hugging black T-shirts and snug black shorts. On their thighs or shins the girls sported alluring tattoos in the shape of Croatian-Celtic braids, thereby linking their limbs to the Croatian medieval period and the Baška tablet—the symbol of Croatian literacy. The young men, unlike the young women, tended to prefer tattoos with more virulent imagery, such as swords piercing hearts, thereby linking themselves to Croatian neo-Ustasha iconography.

The mob of, they say, some hundred thousand people (Croatia is a small country, so one hundred thousand is a substantial crowd!) hollered, sang, leaped, chanted, waved banners and flaming torches; perching on the shoulders of their boyfriends, the girls waved Croatian flags. Thompson raised the fever pitch with his throbbing rhythms and lyrics, fusing the massive crowd into a single capillary system, a herd, a tribe, a single thought, a single, mighty pulsating heart. Thompson's songs with their vocabulary of barely twenty words bolstered ethnic self-esteem.[17] An identical vocabulary and design can be found on the "enemy" Serbian side. There, too, the homeland is described as mother, wife, or beloved. (*Oy, Anitsa, Queen of Knin, Oy, Krajina, fairy sprite / hold me close, hold me tight!*) The lyrics, both Serbian and Croatian, promote a love for rocky terrain: Thompson sings of *genes of stone*;

---

17 Miroslav Sikavica made a documentary on the music-based agitprop of the war years (1991–1995): *Louder Than Guns* (*Glasnije od oružja*), 2017.

one of the popular neo-Ustasha portals has the address *Kamenjar. hr*, meaning, roughly: "rockstrewn.hr"; Serbian pop-music calls to arms and patriotic anthems are advertised as *sounds from a rock-strewn terrain*. The appeal of growing up amid rocks, life among the rocks, and nostalgia for rocks, is something that eludes the author of these lines, but this mystical obsession with rocks definitely excites the authors of those verses and their audiences in both Croatia and Serbia. Serbian patriotic *ojkanje* in a pop song is accompanied by the howling of wolves, for the homeland is a land of wolves (*Mountain wolves in their native land keep guard over the old ways*), placing even greater focus on defending the homeland. No gentler is the slogan on the black T-shirts: *God forgives, but HOS does not!* In other words, God might still forgive the Serbs because loving humankind is part of the job description, but members of the Croatian Defense Forces have no such obligation.

There were young people from all over at the spectacular Ustasha concert, Croatian "children" armed with Croatian flags who'd traveled home for the extravaganza from the Western European countries where they now live and work, with their frenzied chants of *Croatia! Croatia! Croatia!* A young Hungarian couple was caught on video. Every year they come to Croatia to celebrate the *Day of Victory and Homeland Thanksgiving* with Croats. Both of them were wearing the black "outfits." The young Hungarian man tried to explain why he was there, but he found putting it into words difficult. He was simply thrilled, apparently, by the sense of community; there are events identical to this in Hungary. Young Hungarians, Czechs, Slovaks, Croats, Serbs, Bulgarians, Greeks—all of them are similar, they like similar design, similar insignia, similar tattoos, the only nuances of difference being whom they choose to hate. As the majority, they hate minorities, so Roma, apparently, hold first place at the top of the hatred ladder. Jews take second place. In Serbia, aside from the Roma, they hate the Croats, but also all of "our Turks"—meaning the Muslims, Albanians, Bosnians. In Bulgaria it's the Turks, in Croatia—it's the Serbs, Jews, people of color, foreigners. And together they all despise homosexuals. Homosexuals are the red flag for Nazi-males who love their mother-homeland more than their own mothers and wives. They are not homophobic, they claim, but they are also not cowards; they beat up every gay person they come across. In front of the media and news cameras they are more cautious. One T-shirt was particularly inventive. In big font its designer had written: *Ostashe*—both a punning reference to the "Ustashas" and a word meaning "they stayed behind"—then under that, the letter *U* (short for "Ustasha," but also the preposition "in"), and below that, in smaller font: *Croatia*. Below all of the above, the sentence: "They stayed in Croatia," meaning *They did not get going when the going got rough.*

Hungarian and other European neo-Nazis have an identical appreciation for language games, and they favor the mystery number 88. The letter "H" is the eighth in the alphabet, so two eights = two Hs. The abbreviation HH is shorthand for *Heil Hitler.*

Left-leaning intellectuals, philosophers, and political thinkers see all of this, of course, and all of them do what they can to come up with apt names for similar phenomena throughout Europe. The popular umbrella term of *populism* has been picked apart like one of those smoked and dried Caspian carp, known as *vobla* (*Rutilus caspicus*), which Russian drunks back in Soviet days picked apart with their fingers, sucking the oversalted dried flakes of fish, and washing them down generously with beer. And while tasteful left-leaning politicians weigh and gauge these new political, social, and cultural constellations, the local neo-fascists and neo-Nazis are having loads of fun and are showing their frank intention to have loads more fun in the near future.

12.

Meanwhile, during July and August festivities celebrating one thing or another in 2018, the "refugee crisis" was escalating. The Croatian police soon wearied of exercising restraint and embraced a more intimate form of communication with the refugees. This situation resulted in skyrocketing the number of refugees who'd been killed, beaten, robbed (Croatian police stole their money and cell phones), and the story found its way to the "mean-spirited" reporters at *The Guardian*. The Syrians, Afghanis, and Iranians showed the English cameras their bruises, but the Croatian police stood firmly by the claim that the accusations were false, that the migrants were "clashing among themselves and injuring each other." An attractive young man from Syria was interviewed by a reporter. In eloquent English he explained how in Velika Kladuša, on the Bosnian side of the border with Croatia, where an impromptu refugee camp has sprung up, he tried to find a job, but everyone he contacted sent him packing with the same phrase, sweeping him away as if with a verbal broom: *There is nothing! There is nothing! There is nothing!* The Syrian, not without a spark of a humor, declared for the cameras in the language of his hosts (using a phrase that is the identical in Bosnian, Croatian, and Serbian): *Tu nema ničeg—There's nothing here.*

13.

At the new Zagreb airport (yet another institution with the name of Franjo Tuđman, modestly linking Franjo Tuđman to Charles de Gaulle and John F. Kennedy), I am waiting for a flight to Amsterdam. One cannot claim there is *nothing* at the airport, but the space does still yawn half-empty. There are none of the consumer attractions found at other airports. The Zagreb Airport—more for a lack of ideas, it would seem, than by deliberate design—breathes with the ascetic feel of Scandinavian airports. This is why, when I first saw them, I liked the large ads with the slogan *Come Home from Zagreb with a Smile*, until a second later I realized that these were ads designed to attract potential customers for dental tourism. The slogan placed many things in a pragmatic perspective.

People in the know have realized that survival in Croatia, but also anywhere else in the world, lies in offering services. The whole world is connected by a single activity—the exchange of services. Most of us are servicing one another. Women and men working as dentists, hairstylists, pedicurists, cosmeticians, plastic surgeons, personal trainers, masseuses, therapists, waitstaff, hotel staff, sex industry workers, and many others, they are globally interlinked and networked, they are all givers and receivers of services. After all, didn't the Croats expel the Serbs from Krajina so that they themselves could become Krajina dwellers, the defenders of the "bulwark of Christianity"? And judging by the fresh reports from *The Guardian*, they have been doing their job efficiently, even overshooting the expected norm.

Croats earnestly provide Italians with dental implants, while Austrians prefer to go to Hungary or Slovakia for their teeth. Those who have less in their bank accounts head eastward to Bulgaria and Romania. Zagreb and Rijeka compete with Budapest. Belgrade is cheaper, they say, so many are shifting their destinations. Sofia, they say, is cheaper still. Turkey is the new mecca. You can get everything there, a tourist there can get implants, a cataract removed, a hip replacement, meanwhile refurbishing their wardrobe with inexpensive yet high-quality leather goods.

The new Croatian educational system also seems to be turning to servicing. The political elites, the church, and the military are the bedrock on which many countries rely, as does the Croatian state, and all that remains is to shape citizens who will unconditionally support them, the bedrock. Most Croatian children obediently attend vocational secondary schools, meaning that Croatia will soon be a nation of waiters, pedicurists, physical therapists, masseuses, police, priests, and politicians (this last group is the least expensive, no schooling necessary). Young Croats have a choice: they may either leave Croatia and work in Ireland as waiters, pedicurists, physical therapists, or masseuses, or they can stay in Croatia and succumb, like the hillside stripped bare near Petrinja. Things will be as they will be, with us or without us. We must relax and let the water sweep us along . . .

14.

An internet search on the words *Vilina Vlas, Višegrad* will first
bring you to hotel sites, and then words and phrases will come
up such as: *spa, wellness, rehabilitation center, warm thermal waters,
pristine nature, pine forests, five kilometers outside of Višegrad,* and,
of course, photographs of swimming pools, hotel rooms, patients
receiving treatment, and men in white lab coats, there to give
the visitor a feeling of trust. Before Yugoslavia fell apart, the
town of Višegrad had a majority Muslim population, but today
the townspeople are mostly Serbs, and the town is part of the
region known as Republika Srpska, the Serbian part of Bosnia
and Herzegovina. At the entrance to Višegrad stands a brand-
new mosque, built with funding from the European Union, but
clearly there are very few people going in and out. The mosque
stands like a sort of hapless apology, which the European Union
foisted, through their funding, on the local authorities. During
the recent war, the Muslim inhabitants of Višegrad were brutally
liquidated, forced out of their homes, or simply moved away. The
hotel's name, "Vilina Vlas," means "fairy's hair" and it stands on a
spot where water fairies were thought to congregate. Other bodies of water are linked to similar tales. It served, during the war,
as a concentration camp and a "bordello." Dozens and dozens of
young local women were raped there (the precise number is not
known), and there are testimonies and evidence to confirm this.
Serbian paramilitary forces (the White Eagles, Wolves, Aveng-
ers, and others) ran a brutal campaign of ethnic cleansing here.
Many victims met their death in the realm of the water fairies:
the Drina River, Perućac Lake . . . Jasmina Ahmetspahic, a young
woman who could not bear the multiple rapes, threw herself from

a hotel window. Her remains were found when Perućac Lake was drained.

His many male sympathizers call Milan Lukić the "hero of Višegrad," and "white eagle," while at the International Criminal Tribunal for the former Yugoslavia he is called a war criminal. He and his "Eagle" buddies locked 65 Muslims in a house—women, children, and men—on Pioneer (!) Street in Višegrad, and set fire to it. He burned another 70 people alive in another house, also in Višegrad. This same Lukić built his "heroic" reputation on the violent coercion, rape, and sexual humiliation of women at the Vilina Vlas Hotel. The hotel was privatized after the war. Today it is being run as a "rehabilitation center," as it was during the time of Yugoslavia. Its gruesome history has now been erased, though not altogether: the story about the ghastly hotel-bordello has been told by Jasmila Žbanić in her film *For Those Who Can Tell No Tales*, and actress Kym Vercoe wrote the play *Seven Kilometres North-East* about it. There are a few private inns near the hotel, whose proprietors make their living on the fringes of the town's "spa tourism." The names of the inns were either chosen out of a graceless sympathy for the women who were raped, or out of wanton cynicism. One is called *Bambola* (exactly like that: in Italian), while another is called *Memory* (exactly like that: in English).

15.

I recently visited Mirogoj cemetery when I was in Zagreb. My brother, his two children, and I often follow the same path to our family graves, where our parents and my brother's wife are buried.

Aside from the imposing arcades, where lie the great and the rich (perhaps this should go the other way around, the rich and the great), Mirogoj is known for its rolling hills, trees, and greenery, and beautifully arranged graves. This time I noticed that several tombstones had been smashed, something I hadn't noticed before. On these stones there were Serbian first and last names. I saw something like this, as a consequence of Nazi barbarism, at Judischer Friedhof, the abandoned Berlin cemetery on Schonhauser Allee. Strategies of sending messages to the enemy—vandalizing graves, churches, monuments, towns, objects of symbolic importance, and burning books—were and still are used by the many parties to the "Yugoslav conflict" with the same hate-filled verve, although the war was officially over in 1995.

Departures (2008) is a cinematic masterpiece by director Yōjirō Takita. The central protagonist is Daigo Kobayashi, a cellist in a Tokyo orchestra. His orchestra is disbanded, and Daigo and his wife are forced to return to the home Daigo inherited from his mother in a provincial town in the north of Japan. Daigo responds to an ad for work related to "departures," thinking it's a job for a travel agency. Instead, the ad is for a person who will handle departures to "the afterlife" and master the skill of *nōkanshi*, a traditional Japanese ritual for burying the dead. The people who used to do this, because of their work with the deceased, were socially ostracized and stigmatized, because death, the dead, and work with dead bodies, was considered "impure." Daigo endured the painful process of being trained and acclimating to the unpleasant job, followed by obsessive washing and the feeling that the smell of the bodies trailed everywhere after him. Daigo briefly leaves his wife. She is ashamed of his job and sees him—as many from his community do—as "impure." Using oppositions of pure–impure, earth–heaven, physical–spiritual, Yōjirō Takita builds an entire web of metaphors. The many *nōkanshi* repetitions in the movie (the washing, cleaning, dressing the dead body in a ceremonial kimono, or in the late person's favorite clothes, cosmetics, hair, restoring their appeal—always in front of the members of the late person's family) brings closer to death the participants in the ritual: Daigo, his wife, the deceased's family, and—the moviegoers. Daigo refines his craft at *nōkanshi*. And though he sold his expensive instrument after the orchestra was disbanded, he plays every bit as beautifully on his childhood cello.

The art of living, the art of dying, the art of burial, the art of music, the art of understanding, the art of reading . . . While watching the movie, I thought about how Yugoslavia, the country where I was born and grew up, has still not been properly laid to rest. Maybe that is the reason for the barbaric way that the Yugoslav "corpse" has been savaged by the vultures for going on thirty years; they never desist. They aren't all vultures, there is a handful of "musicians" here from the disbanded orchestra who have found work at the funeral home. We "musicians" are ostracized by most of our community. We are doing our best to juggle two skills, the one we've always wanted to master (art), and the other, which life has set before us as a moral imperative. This second skill makes us more responsible and humane, or at least we flatter ourselves that it does. Most of our community goes on avoiding us: we are embroiled in "impure" work and most of the time we carry with us whiffs of the dead.

16.

And while I wait for my flight to Amsterdam, I think my decision to "let the water sweep me along" was not half bad. According to Slavic folk beliefs, the banya is semantically ambivalent: ritual births, ritual funerals, and ritual fortune-telling sessions—readings of the future, are all held there. The *banya* is a site of both spiritual purifying and impurifying, where we wash away impurities, cleanse ourselves of sin, exorcize evil spirits, but also expose ourselves to them. (The *bannik*, an evil spirit, and the *obderiha*, a terrible witch, are *banya* denizens). According to Slavic pagan beliefs, *live* water, *dead* water, *silent* water, all these waters possess magic powers. I can't say whether my spine benefited from my sojourn to the spa, but I do know that this palimpsest—cobbled together from elements of postcommunism, Slavic pagan beliefs about water, the erasure of one history by the imposition of another, wellness and well-being, brute savagery, the vicious hunt for migrants, and a few other odds and ends—makes no sense at all. How many parallel realities, past and current, can there fit in a place where there is nothing? In an attempt to process this tangle of meanings, staring at the global eudaimonic well-being map on my laptop screen, I begin to feel that places of memory are deeply bound to places of forgetting. And doesn't that make sense? The view from my room at the Top-Terme Hotel in Topusko over the outdoor pool in the morning mist—the warm steam billowing up from the water's surface, with the heads of the sparse swimmers only barely visible through the vapor—gave no hint as to whether the scene was of hell or of paradise. It could be both. Paradise, and hell.

17.

"Oh, you absolutely must go see that show!" declare a few of my
compatriots who now live in New York. I catch a particular tenor
to their remark, a patronizing touch, as if they, my compatriots,
are somehow personally responsible for *Toward a Concrete Utopia:
Architecture in Yugoslavia, 1948–1980*, an exhibition currently on
at MoMA. I note the same prideful look that lit up the faces
of Croats when the Croatian national team took second place at
the FIFA World Cup, or of Serbs every time Djokovic plays tennis. "You absolutely must go see that show!" declare a few of my
compatriots, their tone tinged with a scolding edge, as if the very
architects whose work is being exhibited at the show are their
close relatives, and as if I am displaying an unconscionable lack
of enthusiasm for it. "You absolutely must go see that show," they
say. Who knows, maybe some of them voted for Trump, support
his policies, just as they supported Milošević or Tuđman back
home, and today with their righteous tone they're declaring that
I must see this show. Many of them today enjoy the advantages
of life in America and regularly pop back to visit their relatives in
Serbia, bringing back plum brandy to the United States (nowhere
is it as good as it is in Serbia), or to see their relatives in Croatia,
bringing back with them Dalmatian grappa (the "world's finest").
The émigré alphabet is the same everywhere.

At the entrance to the show, the first thing I see is a red kiosk,
the work of Slovenian designer Saša J. Mächtig. This kiosk,
dubbed *K67*, was in use from one end of Yugoslavia to the other,
"from Slovenian Triglav to Macedonian Đevđelija." It played a

number of roles: a newspaper kiosk, a sundries shop, a pastry vendor, a customs office, a hotdog vendor using funny slogans like "Hot Dogs in Warm Buns." The red kiosk hits me with a blast of emotion. The next thing to hit me is the Iskra telephone (I had one just like that!), the wooden chairs, the portable TV (we had one at home!). In one of the darkened halls they are showing an old (from the 1980s?) documentary about hotel architecture, at a time when lavish concrete hotels with swimming pools were being built up and down the Adriatic Coast, when the life portrayed on tourism posters was real and affordable for most. The images come from a life that, with each new day, promised that things would be getting better and better. That life was my life. And it really did get better with each new day.

The film runs on a loop, there is no end or beginning, the end is the beginning, the beginning the end. The museumgoers wander in and out, but I sit there on the wooden bench, in the darkened room, transfixed. I cannot move. The coolness of the room is welcome, the day outside is hot, mid-September (a New York September), I sit there as if in some sort of lavish tomb, where flashes of my former life are being projected onto the wall . . .

Information about the current state of the masterpieces of Yugoslav modernist architecture are muted. The fact that nothing is left standing today but abandoned, devastated ruins of many of the hotels and monuments described in the show, is not exactly concealed, but it is certainly not in the spotlight. The curators were, apparently, reluctant to broach the *befores* and *afters*. That would have been a different story, a story that would have come with strings attached. Still, I was overwhelmed by a rush of gratitude: nothing had been forgotten, there were models on display of the original buildings that have now been largely destroyed, but there you have it, a souvenir model of Bakić's magnificent monument shone there before me in all its stainless steel splendor . . .

18.

One of my countrymen with a New York address, one of the ones who urged me, in that patronizing tone, to see the MoMA exhibition, said . . .

"I am not a fan of women writers . . ."

He is testing me, eyeing me slyly. It goes without saying that my former countryman reads no male writers either, but with that admixture of arrogance and ignorance I know so well he jumps straight into the conversation. He won't spend a dime on my book, he borrows it from a woman friend, waves it around in the air as if any minute now he'll toss it into the corner. He is the legal offspring of a culture that has cooked up brutal jokes about its intellectuals (Have you read Andrić's *Woman from Sarajevo*? Read her? Fucked her! Have you read *Bridge on the Drina*? Read it? Walked it!), he is a product of the culture that devastated the Vojin Bakić monument, he is the child of the culture and, in his chiding tone, he informs me that I really must go see the exhibition at MoMA, but it never occurs to him to pay $10 to a future fund for renovating the monument. Stubborn, pigheaded, illiterate, a servant if so required, rowdy when the opportunity presents itself, a murderer as the occasion demands, a rapist when nobody's watching—he is one of those people who is always right . . .

"I am not a fan of women writers . . ."

"Have you ever actually read a book by a woman writer?"

"Nope, never. Not my cup of tea . . ." he says and sneers.

19.

The photographs I took with my iPhone in the Petrova Gora hills, the ones of the Bakić monument—and only those—are gone. I don't know how it happened. All the other pictures I took are still there. At almost exactly the same instant when I discovered the pictures of the Bakić monument were missing, somebody sent a link to my email of a video, *Darkside*, by Alan Walker, a music producer, a popular twenty-one-year-old "kid." Walker makes abundant use of the visually arresting Yugoslav "concrete utopia" in his video—Dušan Džamonja's *Monument to the Revolution* on Podgarić, the *Monument to the Fallen Partisans* by Miodrag Živković at Tjentište, and the Njegoš mausoleum on Mount Lovćen. Walker's choice in future scenography is, I assume, thanks to photographs taken by Belgian photographer Jan Kempenaers, the first to draw the world's attention to the devastated Yugoslav monuments in his exhibitions and book. Walker reimagines the meaning of the monuments in his video by introducing the imaginary of his generation, rooted in video games, sci-fi props, young people dressed in black-and-white robes with weird cloth masks (bearing Walker's monogram). This semantically vague hodgepodge is flirting with somebody else's semantic system, much the way the kids do who send jokey Instagrams from their tour of Auschwitz. This twofold invalidation fills me with horror. The first one comes from the countries that have come out of Yugoslavia; some of them, while erasing

Yugoslavia, have also erased the country's legacy of anti-fascism, meanwhile destigmatizing fascism (particularly in Croatia). The second invalidation comes from these ignoramuses who, for their "art games," are dusting off whatever they feel like plucking from the world's cultural trash heap.

The Goli Otok prison camp held political prisoners from 1949 to 1956, nominally for their "political reeducation" but in fact it was a Yugoslav gulag, a place far more brutal than a mere reeducation center. After Yugoslavia fell apart, people from the neighboring islands stripped the camp of everything that could be stripped and trashed all they could trash. For a time the ravaged landscape with its abandoned prison cells, shattered windows, and bed-steads strewn around served as the backdrop for gay porn filmed in Croatian–Hungarian coproductions. Then the local tradesmen took things into their own hands and organized modest tourist arrangements: a tour of the island, lunch at the little restaurant by the ferry dock, and the sale of souvenirs. The souvenir that caught my eye was a large wooden bludgeon, and carved in it the friendly words: *Greetings from Goli Otok.*

Attracted by the Brutalist chic of the Yugoslav anti-fascist monuments, the Australian eyewear company Valley Eyewear recently filmed an advertisement video titled *The Happening.* In the video, the exalted models, sunglasses perched on noses, strolled around in front of Bogdan Bogdanović's monument at Jasenovac, the infamous World War II death camp. After cries of outrage in the Serbian media, Valley Eyewear apologized, and for the new backdrop of their ad chose the Bulgarian site of Buzludzha, an example of Bulgarian modernist Brutalist utopian architecture.

Bulgaria, Albania, Romania, in fact all of postcommunist Europe, has ample concrete to spare. It turns out that anti-fascism is as fragile as a crystal glass, perhaps because postcommunist Europe was flooded with ponderous concrete anti-fascist monuments that resemble, from above, a herd of dead elephants.

20.

"I am so glad your back is feeling better and that you've arrived safe and sound on our American shores. While you are in New York, do try out the Korean-run spa in Queens. They have excellent masseuses and a jacuzzi . . ." writes a young acquaintance of mine. He came to the States as a refugee from Bosnia when he was a child; today he teaches early English literature at an American university. I go online, Google the address, search for it on the map, it's not far, I think, and I jot down the phone number. I'll call them tomorrow and make an appointment . . . That life goes on is one of those many comforting banalities. Banalities are comforting because they have the ring of truth. And, indeed, life always does go on.

September 2018

An Archeology of Resistance!?

On I go through the noisy streets (. . .) with every bale I've compacted that day fading softly and quietly inside me. I have a physical sense of myself as a bale of compacted books, the seat of a tiny pilot light of karma, like the flame in a gas refrigerator, an eternal flame I feed daily with the oil of my thoughts, which come from what I unwittingly read during work in the books I am now taking home in my briefcase.

Bohumil Hrabal, *Too Loud a Solitude*

1.

The tale of Scheherazade is one of the cruelest stories about beauty and the importance and vitality of artistic expression. It tells of the relationship between the artist and authority, suggesting that the creative act itself is an act of resistance; it conveys the message that there can be no authentic artistic act without personal risk. Although one of the oldest, the legend of Scheherazade is an unlikely choice for the artistic resistance corpus. Might that be because at the heart of the metaphor stands a woman who, by telling stories saves not only her own life, but the lives of the future victims of Shahryar the misogynist? Does the story's happy end compromise the gravity of Scheherazade's resistance? After Scheherazade's storytelling marathon, which lasts a thousand and one nights, Shahryar falls in love with her. The storyteller and her potential executioner go on to live together. Scheherazade's victory is also her greatest defeat: Shahryar may have given up on cutting off women's heads, but misogyny—surprise, surprise—is still flourishing.

The myths and legends about artistic creativity are most often romantic, although the same can't be said for the practice of life. The artist is shaking up God's order and this is why he must be punished. The punishment is more draconian if the "artist" is a woman. With their act of creativity, the artist is unconsciously vying with God. Artistic creativity implies undermining the entrenched system of values—aesthetic, moral, political—and bringing in a new vision of the world. The contemporary "creative industry" has erased these romantic clichés, replacing them with clichés about more pragmatic and comprehensible forms of artistic success.

2.

I remember my childhood as a time of repressive channeling from the surrounding community, of exposure to the terror of popular "generalities." Out of an understandable desire not to have their child stand apart from the rest of the community, my parents went along, tacitly, with this "channeling." *Moderation in all things*. This popular axiom advised cleaving to the median; in other words: mediocrity. Adaptation to societal norms was the most remunerative and secure life choice. *Who flies high, falls low.* This proverb clipped my wings, and scared and attracted me in equal measure. The saying *Don't lock horns with hornéd beasts* taught obedience, admitting the power of those stronger, advocating submission to all forms of authority. In the community where I grew up it was not advisable to raise one's voice. *Silence is golden.* Silence, hypocrisy, and lies were the ways one evaded all sorts of trouble.

Unlike my community, my parents' life choices did challenge the rule of the golden mean. When World War II broke out, my father, at seventeen, joined the Partisans. After the war he worked for a *bright future*, a society where nobody would be hungry, humiliated, or despised, and his legacy was a modest heap of worthless medals given him for his *dedicated work at building a socialist Yugoslavia*. He fell in love with my mother, a woman from another country, during a dangerous and, fortunately, brief period when relationships with foreigners were tantamount to treason. A deep-seated resistance to the terror visited upon me by this community, which set the moral, aesthetic, and other standards while brimming with self-righteous sanctimony, my love for my parents who, whether they meant to or not, marked me with a sense of "other-ness," and my early passion for literature—all these were my signposts. Greek myths, Partisan legends, Hollywood films, and fairy tales, especially the tale of courageous youth Danko, a sort of communist Jesus Christ, who ripped his own heart from his chest to light the way with it, and lead people out from the dark forest into a sunny clearing. This modest cultural package bolstered inside me the first parameters of good and evil.

3.

Today, I often feel I grew up and lived in one time and then found myself, suddenly, in another. In any case, the fairy tale about the courageous youth Danko would probably elicit sneers today, which, it should be said, Maxim Gorky, the author of the tale, also anticipated: as soon as they step out into the sunny clearing, a scoundrel stomps on Danko's pulsing heart as if it were a frog. The culture of the heart has long since been elbowed out by the culture of money. The truths we knew have been undone and replaced by new truths. In the small country of Croatia where I was born, three thousand monuments—which were raised after World War II to commemorate the Yugoslav resistance movement, the Partisans—have been demolished over the last twenty-five years or so. An army of unqualified historians is toiling today, erasing antifascist history and legalizing revisionist historical versions.

The Polish Institute for National Remembrance, with quite a crew of diligent staffers, is toiling to expunge all guilt from the collective conscience of the Polish people by erasing it from the national historical record and the history books. The Polish courts are now under the total control of the government, and the Polish Senate has approved what is popularly known as the Holocaust law. Those who use the phrase "Polish death camps" can be prosecuted in court. For on "occupied" Polish territory, the death camps were, they claim, built by the *Nazis*, with whom the *blameless* Poles had no connection whatsoever. And in Croatia, as well as Serbia, many are toiling to sanctify the criminals, the ones from World War II and the new ones from the *recent* war. Today, in the heart of Europe, in Bosnia and Herzegovina, Croatian, Bosnian, and Serbian children are required to attend ethnically separated classrooms; they study the same history and the same language but from completely different textbooks. News of similar approaches has also been heard from Hungary, Bulgaria, Greece, Lithuania, the Czech Republic, Slovakia, Macedonia, and in Europe's north and south, east and west, and these currents are merging into a subterranean river that is slowly but surely eroding the ideological and ethical foundations on which Europe stands, foundations built on the rubble of World War II.

4.

My late mother was haunted her whole life by images of what she saw in 1946 when she traveled from Sofia by train through southern Serbia and Belgrade on her way to Zagreb . . . "Everything was rubble!" she'd say, always with the same incredulity and the same shudder. There were no images conveyed by that sentence, and I wasn't able to picture the reality this sentence described. Today, twenty years after the *recent* war (this being the name that has taken root in the language, yes, the *recent war*, 1991–1995) I feel as if I do know. For twenty years I have been living in rubble. And yet, nobody has established a reckoning of the damages. How many people killed, how many disappeared, how many displaced, how many economically ruined, how many houses demolished, how many factories destroyed, how many miles of railway lines, roads, hospitals, churches, schools, monuments ravaged, how many books burned . . . Nobody has yet offered a summation. The authorities in most of the ex-Yugoslav statelets are not interested in either a reckoning or a renewal, all they care about is maintaining the status quo, a limbo between war and peace, between devastation and revitalization. All they care about is process, collapse, slow motion. So court proceedings drag on for years. So houses are undergoing permanent repairs, yes, but people don't move in because there's always some key part missing, a roof, door, windows . . . Reforms are promised but not implemented. War criminals, murderers, thieves are not convicted, and even if they're sentenced, they don't do their time behind bars. Life mid-rubble is a process, a continuing condition. For only in this manner can those survive who produced the rubble, those who supported them, and those who did absolutely nothing to prevent them. It's as if they are not people but cogs in the machine of destruction, the machine of self-destruction.

Where lies the appeal of fascism and its many forms, soaking into Europe like ink into a dry blotter? It lies in the fact that fascism requires no qualifications, no guarantees, no certification of any specific education or knowledge. Fascism's appeal lies in belonging to a like-minded group of people, in acceptance, in the violence of one gang over another, in the easily stoked feeling that we're better than others, we're finally better, and being better— surprise, surprise—doesn't take much, only the same blood group and a willingness to do violence to those who don't share that blood group with you.

5.

In Vodice, a tourist town on the Adriatic coast, Croatian "volunteers," or veterans of the *recent* war, viciously ransacked flowerbeds in a local park in late April 2018. These "valiant" Croatian veterans had the impression, apparently, that the flower beds were laid out in the provocative shape of the "aggressor's" five-pointed star. The red star, the symbol of Communism, has the same effect on segments of the Croatian population as the *red flag* does on a bull. The flower beds, protested the mayor, were arranged like a five-petalled blossom, not a five-pointed star.

In late October, Zagreb photographer Robert Gojević mounted a show of twelve large-format photographs along the central walkway through Maksimir, Zagreb's largest park. The show was conceived of as an homage to Ivan Standl, the Zagreb photographer who first memorialized Maksimir. The exhibit was scheduled to travel after this to other Croatian parks. Only a few hours after the photographs were put up, they were slashed to pieces.

Several days later, in early November, a drunk in Split lunged at one of the few monuments still standing from the Partisan movement, one to Rade Končar, a war hero. The sculpture toppled more easily than he'd expected and fell onto the drunken vandal, breaking his leg. The vandal ended up in the hospital, and he used the opportunity to tell journalists that he had nothing against the "fellow himself" (meaning Rade Končar, shot in 1942), he knew nothing about the man, but in principle he couldn't stand those "Serbs, Partisans, and Communists."

And so, day by day, a quarter century has passed. I chose these three recent incidents at random; any three would have sufficed, each exemplifying a form of violence. Such violence is now the norm. Any political justification for the murder, theft, and brutal violence—like the drunken wretch who despises "Serbs, Partisans, and Communists" or the men who despised the flowerbeds, thinking they were a five-pointed star—is moot. Everything can become an object of violence: a theater performance and its director, a literary work and its author, a photographer and his politically innocent photographs. Fascism loves a void. Fascism loves death. Perhaps this is why ever more numerous, ugly, and monumental sculptures are being raised in the most vacant, parched, barren, devastated places to the "father of the Croatian nation," Franjo Tuđman, the first Croatian president (the most recent of these sculptures stands 15 feet tall, and once the pedestal is added, it will tower at over 22 feet), and streets, parks, institutions, airports, squares are being given new names, most of them "Franjo Tuđman," a perfect confirmation of the catastrophic deficit of other substance. The selection of the symbolic subject— Tuđman and only Tuđman—does away with any dilemma about choice. There is only one *Bible* for the choosing, one church, one religion, one ideology, one race, one class. The Sacred One is the haven of the illiterate.

6.

Sophophobia is the term used for fear of knowledge and learning. Among many of my compatriots I note apathy, lethargy, a striking absence of curiosity, reliance on stereotypes, a refusal for anything that would require them to step outside their familiar world. The knowledge, long since embraced, that the world is round is now gradually giving way to the more ancient knowledge that Earth is a flat disk. This rigidity of human minds was duly noted by the first experts who attempted to draw the attention of young amateur Wikipedia editors to their inaccuracies and errors. The complaints were seldom taken on board.

The catastrophic plummet in educational standards began with the collapse of Yugoslavia, the upsurge of nationalism, the massive layoff of journalists, doctors, judges, all of whom—or at least this was the way it played out in Croatia—were Serbs, non-Croats, former Communists, or simply people critical of the system of corruption in the new states. The plummet of all standards began with nepotism, with the vast power of the church, with the law by which Croats, veterans, the children of veterans, patriots—but not experts—were favored in the hiring process.

This class of illiterates was described the most succinctly, precisely, and vibrantly by Mikhail Zoshchenko in 1923 in his little satirical story, "The Lady Aristocrat." Grigory Ivanovich is a janitor, a plumber, who tells of his brief, unsuccessful relationship with a "lady aristocrat." The semi-literate janitor, who has never been to the theater, takes the lady aristocrat to a play. Zoshchenko benevolently derides the class of people who were victorious with the revolution and ushered in revolutionary populism along with their notions of culture, beauty, education, life, values. Each time I see the new post-Yugoslav fascist class in the media flaunting their expensive name-brand clothes, beautified by cosmetic interventions, their little lap poodles, attending all the fashion shows, first nights at the theater, and art openings, when I see the exemplars of that class giving voice to their critiques of the theaters, books, art shows, I think of Zoshchenko. While Zoshchenko mocked the cultural literacy of his day, today's Croatian elite actually enjoys theirs, and in the power and profit their ignorance brings them.

7.

The exhibit *The Archeology of Resistance: Discovering Collections of Cultural Opposition in Socialist Croatia* opened in Zagreb in October 2018. It came about as a collaborative effort between the Croatian Institute of History and the Croatian State Archives, as part of the European project known, for short, as COURAGE, or, in full: *Cultural Opposition—Understanding the Cultural Heritage of Dissent in the Former Socialist Countries.* On the list of participants in the Courage project is Budapest, with its best research institutes, three of them, which somehow implies that if there were to be a massive flood, only the Hungarian version of history would end up the right one: it would be at a statistical advantage. The others listed are: Vilnius, Prague, Bucharest, Zagreb, Bratislava, and institutions of higher learning in Oxford, Dublin, and Regensburg. The project was generously funded by the European Community.

The curators of the exhibit were guided by the grand notion that every resistance is, plain and simple, resistance, every opposition is, plain and simple, opposition, and all the totalitarianisms can be lumped together (which, is, by the way, the most hostile, egregious, and mendacious ideological malarkey in the post-Yugoslav ideological zone, and beyond). This approach promotes the notion that human history is an ash heap of debris where all of us end up: "émigrés, the faithful, dissidents, Praxis members, youth, artists, feminists, censors, ideologists, secret agents," because ultimately we're all the same, the good and the bad, the right and the wrong, Hitler and Jesus Christ. Every act of resistance is, therefore, pointless because we will all be a pile of bones in the end, which a future ideologue will attempt to *reconcile*. Interesting that the Catholic Church, the most powerful institution among Croats, didn't protest at having their icon, Bishop Alojzije Stepinac, who endorsed the Ustasha regime, relegated to the same ash heap as Tomislav Gotovac, the Croatian conceptual artist who, for his performances, was wont to strip down naked and kiss the Zagreb pavement.

8.

This freshest example of Croatian historical revisionism and the strategies of a determined destigmatizing of the Ustasha movement, the Ustasha Independent State of Croatia and its infamous leader Ante Pavelić, of denying the existence of the Nazi camps in Croatia, as well as of denying the atrocities committed by Croats during the *recent* war, takes us back to a different time and place. The 1943 attack on the *Amsterdams Bevolkingsregister* (the Amsterdam civil registry office) to destroy the registries that the Nazis could use to identify Jews has remained etched in the collective consciousness of the people of the Netherlands as a shining example of resistance to Nazi terror. A group of artists risked their own lives to save the lives of fellow citizens. There exists, of course, the other dark, parallel history, the history of collabora-tion. The case of Anne Frank unites both, the light and the dark. Anne Frank is a story of resistance, but also of betrayal.

At the site of the Museum of Resistance (*Verzetsmuseum*) in Amsterdam the visitor is met with the following unambiguous question in several languages: "Nazi Germany has occupied Hol-land. What will you do?" and three possibilities, three answers, three buttons to press:

AANPASSEN. MEEDOEN. VERZETTEN.
ADAPT. COLLABORATE. RESIST.
ANPASSEN. MITMACHEN. WIDERSTEHEN.
S'ADAPTER. COLLABORER. RESISTER.

When the war began in 1991 in destabilized Yugoslavia, I clicked on the invisible button: RESIST. VERZETTEN. This was a per-sonal—unpremeditated perhaps, but certainly sincere—act of resistance to the stupidity and lies, a protest against those many, disgraceful strategies by which the future pillagers and murderers set out to convince the people of Yugoslavia that war was a neces-sity and there were no options available other than fratricide.

Several years later, when I turned up in the Netherlands after leaving my country, somebody (apologies for this digression into self-pitying self-praise) recognized my gesture of resistance and gave me the Verzetsprijs in 1997, an award which was still being conferred then in recognition of those Dutch artists who gave their lives during Nazism in defense of human dignity, theirs and their fellow citizens'. This unexpected Dutch welcome was what inspired me to unpack my suitcases and make my new home there. The award, sadly, no longer exists. I was its last recipient. I know now that one presses that imaginary button on an impulse, just as I know that people from all historical constellations most often choose the button AANPASSEN. ADAPT. The survival instinct prevails, and adaptation, they say, guarantees survival. A negligible minority will press the VERZETTEN button. I believe the intelligentsia—the schoolteachers, professors, artists, writers, scholars, journalists, and many others—will stop and think about whether to choose to adapt, collaborate, or to resist overt, covert, and all other forms of terror. These three buttons— adaptation, collaboration, resistance—determine the culture in which we live, the political, literary, artistic, educational, media culture of everyday life, as well as what that culture will be like tomorrow. Literally, tomorrow. Ex-Yugoslavs have been living that culture, faced with it as with their own face in the mirror, for a full quarter century now, but they still haven't succeeded in coming up with a name for it. In politically less-sensitive times, it would be called post-fascist. Or neofascist. Today, with the full awareness and responsibility of the thinking democratic majority, it is most often termed populist. The word "populism" was the word of the year in 2017. It can be translated as the rule of the illiterate.

9.

Somewhere, among the newspapers offering reviews of the exhibit, *The Archeology of Resistance*, flashed the faces of the curators, a young man with an innocent, round face and blue gaze expressing nothing, and a young woman on whose face the camera caught an unpleasantly cunning expression. While I studied these smooth, right-thinking faces, I was struck by the thought these are *they*, the angels of death, my future executioners, this is what they look like, they have infiltrated the key state institutions, the archives, the international networks, and receive generous subsidies from numerous commissions populated by similar angels, who, with their invisible wings, are cleansing and discarding everything that is to be thrown away, everything that no longer has a purpose and all this together, all human effort, will be tossed onto the ash heap. Before the cold heavens there is no such thing as right or wrong, and all our efforts are in vain. I studied the photograph of these two young angels with their indifferent faces and wondered how many more there are like them . . . Tens? Hundreds? Hundreds of thousands?

10.

An archeology of resistance!? Has resistance now been relegated to archeological digs? Does this mean that we are truly denizens in the ash heap of historical debris, we're historical debris but haven't yet understood this to be so? Or have we? The archive and archivization, "archive fever," the museum and musealization, the past and a "better past" are the vocabulary of the present, while the word *future* vanished along with Harrison "Jack" Schmitt, the most recent astronaut to walk on the moon, or, somewhat later, with Fukuyama's fatal pronouncement about the end of history.

We are plagued by the feeling that everything is slipping too fast through our fingers. Thanks to the help of seductive technology, we have recast our fear of death into the ritual of the daily archiving of our lives, from snapping pictures of what we're eating for dinner with friends to pictures of our own bare ass, which we snap at exotic destinations and send off to the networked world, so our friends, family members, and random curiosity-seekers can be sure that we and our ass are, thank goodness, alive and mobile. And the more technological toys there are to help us register our voice, face, movement, the faster and more efficient the forgetting becomes. We're constantly making trash and then collecting it—these two actions are sometimes out of sync and vie with one another. Sometimes an Instagram egg named Eugene catches our attention and the attention of another fifty million people. We're buried in rubbish, shards, trash, rubble, debris, vestiges of something that, until recently, held meaning and function. Today, our metaphorical home and the surrounding landscape are a garbage dump. We're gradually joining the seagulls and the crows, greedily pulling at somebody's bowels, plastic bags, rags, rotten food . . . We are no longer able to handle the speed, the extreme present, yet we feel as if we haven't even had a chance to be born, but, look, now we're dying. Hence the hysteria of self-archiving and self-musealization which we succumb to without resistance. We send our reflections into the world at top speed as if every day is judgment day and our Instagram simply must appear on God's computer screen. At top speed we nibble at YouTube videos as if they are fast food, and bow down to the sudden revelation of God in the form of Eugene the Egg.

And if somebody in this age, in which we're all swimming in debris, asks me for directions, for what to grab onto to keep from sinking, if someone asks me who the person, point, mental state, ideology, metaphor, religion, utopia, straw, or, simply, consolation would be—Hanta comes immediately to mind.

Hanta is the protagonist and narrator of Bohumil Hrabal's masterpiece *Too Loud a Solitude*. He is a well-read recluse, a social outcast, a "yurodivi," a sacrificial lamb of his time, who has worked for thirty-five years compacting old paper, mainly discarded books. He shapes them into special bales. To each bale he gives "his signature." Into each he builds his heart. He would never pack Kafka and Hitler together in a bale. In the thirty-five years he has been working while surrounded by books, which are like living beings for him, he has been living in "too loud a solitude," he does the work of a "tender butcher," and as the "heavens are not humane," he finds consolation in "compassion and love." All in all *the manuscripts are not burning*. Today, Hanta's offspring are the rising "archeologists," the collectors, navigators, cartographers of memory maps, historians, artists, explorers, memento collectors, those who repair the damage, the builders and rebuilders, the righteous who work on the historical "refuse," the educators, protectors of truth, the curators of virtual museums, the staff working in memory laboratories . . . Thanks to Hanta's children, manuscripts don't burn. And when they're tossed into the bonfire, the books laugh with the "quiet laugh" of resistance.

December 2018

·

Author's Note

The essays in this book were written between 2014 and 2018 and they are given here in chronological order. Some first appeared in print in *Salmagundi* as part of my "Homelands & Exiles" column there, others in *Gazeta Wyborcza* in Poland, *Peščanik*, a Serbian online portal, *World Literature Today*, *Los Angeles Literary Review*, *Exchanges*, *LitHub*, all published in the United States, *Neue Zurcher Zeitung* and *Die Weltwoche* of Switzerland, *De Groene Amsterdammer* and *Nexus* of the Netherlands, and the online journal *Asymptote*. The essay "The Age of Skin" was included in *Pushcart Prize XL 2016*, a prestigious collection of the best literary essays that appeared the previous year with small presses and journals.

The mottoes attributed to Roma fairy tales come from *Lord, Turn Me Into an Ant!*, Belgrade, 2011, a book of fairy tales of the Roma of Kosovo and Metohija. The mottoes attributed to *Primer* were taken from *Primer for the First Grade of the Peoples" School*, Zagreb, 1957.

The English edition doesn't quite match the Croatian edition published with the title *The Age of Skin* (Doba Koze, 2019). I omitted one long essay from the English edition, and included an essay that was originally published as a separate little book: *Tu nema nicega!* [There's Nothing Here!, 2020].

Dubravka Ugresic

Translator's Note

The Isaac Babel motto from "Gapa Gužva" was taken from *The Complete Works of Isaac Babel*, translated by Peter Constantine from the Russian. The motto taken from *Too Loud a Solitude* by Bohumil Hrabal was translated by Michael Henry Heim from the Czech. The passages from Milan Kundera's novels *Slowness* and *Ignorance* were translated from the French by Linda Asher. The translations of the mottoes and verses which are originally in Bosnian, Croatian, and Serbian sources are mine.

Ellen Elias-Bursać, 2019

DUBRAVKA UGRESIC is the author of seven works of fiction, including *The Museum of Unconditional Surrender* and *Baba Yaga Laid an Egg*, along with seven collections of essays, including *Thank You for Not Reading* and *Karaoke Culture*, a finalist for the National Book Critics Circle Award for Nonfiction. She has won, or been shorlisted for, more than a dozen prizes, including the NIN Award, Austrian State Prize for European Literature, Heinrich Mann Prize, *Independent* Foreign Fiction Prize, Man Booker International Prize, and the James Tiptree Jr. Award. In 2016, she received the Neustadt International Prize for Literature (the "American Nobel") for her body of work.

ELLEN ELIAS-BURSAĆ has been translating fiction and nonfiction by Bosnian, Croatian, and Serbian writers since the 1980s, including novels and short stories by David Albahari, Dubravka Ugresic, Daša Drndić, and Karim Zaimović. She is co-author of a textbook for the study of Bosnian, Croatian, and Serbian with Ronelle Alexander, and author of *Translating Evidence and Interpreting Testimony at a War Crimes Tribunal: Working in a Tug-of-War*, which was awarded the Mary Zirin Prize in 2015.

**OPEN
LETTER**

OPEN LETTER

WWW.OPENLETTERBOOKS.ORG